Oxford Castaways

Sylvia Vetta

OXFORDFOLIO

In memory of Rebecca Allison (Castaway 2:39)

An OXFORDFOLIO Book
46 Hayfield Road, Oxford, OX2 6TU
www.oxfordfolio.co.uk

© Sylvia Vetta, 2017

Original jacket design and layout: James Huw King
Additional design, typesetting and photography: Philip Hind
www.philiphind.com

Printed by Latimer Trend

ISBN: 978-0-9956794-0-5

British Library Cataloguing-in-Publication Data

A catalogue record for this book is available from the British Library

All rights reserved. No part of this publication may be reproduced,
stored in a retrieval system, or transmitted in any form or by
any means, electronic, mechanical, photocopying, recording or
otherwise, without the prior written permission of the publisher.
Please contact the publisher for permissions. This book may not be
lent, resold, hired out or otherwise disposed of by way of trade in
any form of binding or cover other than that in which it is published,
without the prior consent of the Publisher.

10 9 8 7 6 5 4 3 2 1

Interviews originally featured in The Oxford Times's
Oxfordshire Limited Edition magazine, with kind permission.

Jacket illustration *Sheldonian* © Dorothy Megaw 2017
www.ohtobee.co.uk

Contents

Acknowledgements 4

Foreword 5

Introduction: The Sobell House Story 7

The Castaways

3:1 Dwina Gibb 20

3:2 Aidan Meller.. 28

3:3 Annie Sloan... 35

3:4 Christopher Brown 43

3:5 Icolyn Smith 50

3:6 Estelle Bailey... 55

3:7 Dennis Harrison.. 63

3:8 Gillian Cox 68

3:9 Don Manley..74

3:10 Georgina Ferry 80

3:11 Jeremy Spafford 86

3:12 Katie Read 93

3:13 Legs Larry Smith 100

3:14 Fiona Carnarvon 108

3:15 Mark Davies 114

3:16 Nancy Hunt 120

3:17 Roger Neill..128

3:18 Zoe Broughton.......................................134

3:19 Qu Leilei 140

3:20 Francesca Kay..148

3:21 Andrew McMichael 153

3:22 Pauline Goddard 160

3:23 Richard O.Smith 166

3:24 & 3:25 Tish Francis and Kim Pickin 171

3:26 Paul Hobson 178

3:27 Yasmin Robson 182

3:28 Richard B Parkinson 187

3:29 Trevor Cowlett 193

3:30 Sylvia Vetta..199

Acknowledgments

Oxfordshire Limited Edition castaway series began in January 2008 and ended in 2016 after nine years of monthly features.

Oxford Castaways 3 is the third and final book bringing together the life stories of the inspirational people I have had the privilege to interview for the series. One of them, Dwina Gibb, has generously covered the production costs of Oxford Castaways 3 which aims to raise awareness of what Sobell House does in Oxfordshire and to ensure that all proceeds from book sales will go to the charity. We begin with six mini features of people who work at the hospice which I hope shines a spotlight on what makes Sobell House so special.

Thanks are due to James Harrison of Oxfordfolio for producing such a beautiful book and for James Huw King who created the cover and interior design. The artwork is by local and very talented artist Dorothy Megaw (www.ohtobee.com).

Thanks to Tim Metcalfe who commissioned the series in 2008 and supported me from 1998 when I began writing for the magazine. Thanks to Jaine Blackman, the current editor of Oxfordshire Limited Edition, who brought the series to an appropriate end with style and sensitivity. Thanks also to Newsquest for allowing the use of the photographs free of charge.

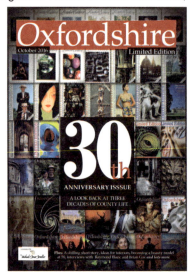

As the final castaway number 120, I too made the choice of art, objects or books to take to Oxtopia. The experience of being interviewed by Philip Hind made me even more appreciative of all the amazing people who have allowed me to interview them. Oxford is a truly international city whose diversity, in my opinion, is not adequately reflected in local media. The image we see is overwhelmingly pale. The delight of the Castaways series has been the diversity of the life stories of people from all over the country and all over the world. Their backgrounds could not be more different but what they have in common is a positive attitude to life and a link to Oxford and to Oxfordshire.

I hope you enjoy dipping in and out of the life stories in Oxford Castaways, Oxford Castaways 2 and now Oxford Castaways 3.

Sylvia Vetta

Foreword

Sobell House is about Life

Like many people I thought a hospice was where you went in your final weeks, but through a friend, Rex Mears, I discovered that Sobell House is also about life. In 1996 I was the director of Oxford Antiques Centre (aka 'The Jam Factory') and Rex's wife Rose ran our bookshop. Aged only fifty-five, Rex was given six months to live. So he paid a visit to Sobell House to find out more about its 18-bed in-patient unit. He thought it could be the place where he would go to die. But he discovered much more than he had expected. He learned about the day services and began attending three days a week. With the pain control and support he received he lived for a further three unexpected years of good quality living.

I visited Lindsay Manifold the Sobell House fundraiser to discuss the possibility of Oxford Castaways 3 being published in support of the hospice. (Lindsay's story is featured later in this book.) She described the difference high quality palliative care can make: "Once symptoms are under control, it enables the patient to live their lives. That is why I like to think of Sobell House as about life."

Sobell House's specialist palliative care nurses take their skills beyond the doors of the hospice and work throughout Oxfordshire hospitals. There is also a team of community nurses who help patients in their own homes.

Rex Mears told me "I thought this was a place where you came and died, and that was it; but at Sobell they have time for you." He described the warm atmosphere where people make friends quickly. It is not solemn and in a way it intensifies your life. Rex learned a new skill – breadmaking and sold the delicious loaves he baked giving the proceeds to the hospice. By the time patients go to Sobell House they know they cannot expect a cure, but many patients say that they no long worry about death. The compassion and sensitive care they receive is remarkable.

I visited the Day Centre and entered a warm, light and cheerful lounge which opens on to a beautiful garden. I met some of the army of volunteers who were working there that day. The volunteers bring with them a multitude of skills and a spirit of empathy. The day I visited, two volunteers were helping with an art activity designed by artist and recent volunteer, Claire Goodall. Claire explained: "There is one part of the garden which is rather dark and the mosaic leaves we are making will form a colourful tree to brighten up the wall. The title of the artwork will evolve but it was inspired by the hospice logo which is an oak tree." Claire believed that art activities can take people out of themselves for a while and can also lead to unexpected conversations.

Someone At Hand to Listen

Volunteers are ready to listen and activities create openings where patients feel able to express their concerns. In the nineteenth century the taboo subject was sex but our Victorian ancestors were comfortable talking about death. In the second half of the twentieth century that all changed. Gradually people in the West became happier talking openly about sex, but death became the taboo subject.

One day we will all face death but few of us are good at talking about it. Once someone is diagnosed with a terminal illness, death is real and immediate but every moment of life becomes important. That is why Lindsay is right when she says Sobell House is about life. Most patients are reluctant to burden their family and friends with their anxieties and fears; they want to enjoy every moment they can with them. But at Sobell House day services they find an opportunity to express themselves. They make friends with other day centres users who are in the same position. The ratio of volunteers and staff to patients is high so, as Rex told me, there is always someone at hand to listen to you.

The Volunteers

The Sobell House volunteers are special people. One of my castaways in Oxford Castaways 2 was the mezzo-soprano and music teacher Rebecca Alison. Rebecca was only 47 when she unexpectedly died of meningitis in 2016. Kennington United Choirs conducted by Trevor Cowlett (whose story also features in this book) performed Mozart's *Requiem* as a tribute to Rebecca. The chaplain of Sobell House told us about a side of Rebecca of which most us knew nothing. The Rebecca we knew sang in concerts and musicals, was active in the community and with youth music theatre. What we didn't know was that on most Fridays she volunteered at Sobell House. Yes she used the piano in the Day Centre and yes she would sometimes burst into song but like all the volunteers she was there to help in any way she could. Volunteers make tea, serve lunch, play cards or chess or just sit in quiet companionship. Rebecca like so many volunteers gave her time and used her talent. Her premature death reminds us that not all terminally ill patients are old and some leave young families.

Sobell House supports bereaved families. Families often need practical help with financial difficulties when facing the prospect of losing a major contributor to the family income. That is why Sobell House employs social workers and a benefit officer. The hospice runs transport facilities sometimes funded by the charity and other times provided free by volunteers.

They offer telephone support through their triage service and ward seven days a week. Sobell House's reputation is world class and that is why it is a place where professionals can come for training and learning about how to offer the highest standards of care for people facing that elephant in the room, the end of life.

Introduction: The Sobell House Story

Celebrating 40 Years of Care

The concept of a hospice is not new. In medieval Europe a hospice or hospital was a refuge for travellers: a place to receive hospitality. Even the Knights Hospitallers (an order of military monks, following chiefly the rule of St. Augustine, which took its origin from a hospital founded at Jerusalem c.1000 by merchants of Amalfi, who provided succour and protection of poor pilgrims visiting the Holy Land) recognised that the dying needed a separate place in their 'hospital' where they could receive special care. In 1967,the world's first purpose-built hospice was established in Sydenham, South East London. St Christopher's became the model for the hospice in its modern sense. Its founder Dame Cicely Saunders recognised the inadequacy of the care of the dying that was offered in hospitals. St Christopher's became a pioneer in the field of palliative medicine.

Hospice Care in Oxford

Writing the Oxford Castaways series I discovered that Oxford has played a significant role in the hospice movement. Cecily Saunders graduated from St. Anne's College Oxford (1938–1939 and 1944–1945). An early castaway was Sister Francis Domenica who founded the world's first hospice for children at Helen and Douglas House in East Oxford. Gillian Cox (who features in this edition) and Steve Corea, the then assistant director of Oxfordshire Mental Health Services spearheaded the foundation of Vale House on Botley Road Oxford in 1990. It is thought that Vale House was the first specialist hospice for the care of people with terminal Alzheimer's. Oxford Castaways 2 was published in support of Vale House.

While Sobell House was not the first modern hospice it has become a beacon for good practice and is respected internationally for its teaching and clinical research. At the time St Christopher's opened its doors, the need for similar specialist end of life care was brought to the attention of the Board of Governors of the then United Oxford Hospitals by Dr Frank Ellis who was a senior consultant radiologist. But it would take ten years for Dr Ellis's wish to come to fruition. He pointed out that many terminally ill patients did not fit the category 'geriatric' care. In those days Geriatric Wards provided the nearest thing to end of life care in the NHS but were not cheerful or homely places. An investigation was commissioned and the report in 1968 confirmed the need for 75 beds in the Oxford area. But the low priority given to it and the lack of funds saw inaction.

Green Roots

Sir Michael Sobell was the president of the National Society for Cancer Relief (which is now best known as Macmillan Cancer Care). He saw the report and was impressed and offered personally to support the building of a 25-bed facility in Oxford.

A site was found on the Churchill Hospital campus. Sir Michael loved trees and gardens and wanted the building to connect to nature and the location made that possible. But the building costs kept rising. Sir Michael generously stepped in and increased his donation to £200,000; the local community raised £50,000 which triggered support from the NHS of £45,000. Forty years ago in 1976, the hospice – named after the generous donor who made it possible – was ready to open its doors.

The aim was for general running costs to be funded by the NHS, with additional services provided by fundraising. Even at zero hour an NHS impending embargo on new projects threatened the opening of Sobell House. Compromises were made with the NHS which meant that just twelve of the beds could be occupied. The first patient was admitted in April 1976. Consultant Radiotherapist Dr Alistair Laing took on the additional and demanding role of Acting Consultant in charge and two other doctors, Dr Richards and Dr Patrick Lawrence, undertook the day to day work. The first member of staff to be appointed was Vivien Pritchard 1975. With two ward sisters, Alison Parry and Jane Harvey (who went to St Luke's Nursing Home in Sheffield for extra training).

Sobell's Ethos

One of the first decisions taken at Sobell House was that staff should be known by their given names in order to give the feeling of a home and not a hospital environment. In his speech at the opening of Sobell House Dr Laing described the needs of the patients who would use the hospice: they are relief from distressing symptoms and from the fear of such symptoms and an environment of caring and of companionship both of the family and the community.

Since 1976, knowledge of techniques of palliative care has improved through research and practice. The charity's education department has the key role in Sobell House's drive to improve the care of the dying in Oxfordshire and to spread learning locally, nationally and internationally. The number of people dying each year is increasing, so hospice care has never been more in demand. Over the next five to ten years Sobell House wants to build the necessary infrastructure to deliver more direct care both in the hospice, the home, the community and in main hospitals. To do that and to maintain services the charity must constantly raise money and are always in search of new donors and supporters.

The role of the community as set out in 1976 is provided by volunteers and by the continuing support of local people. Although in the beginning Sobell House Hospice Charity (previously Friends of Sobell House) was funding 'extras', by the 1990s voluntary funding of around £500,000 was being provided, supporting core services, and this support continues to grow, and currently stands at around £1.5m per year.

Sobell House Castaways

Wanting an insight into life in Sobell House, I suggested casting away a cross section of people who work or volunteer at the hospice. Lindsay Manifold arranged the interviews for me. It seemed a good idea to begin with Lindsay herself because she has worked at the hospice since 1998 as their fundraiser.

Lindsay Manifold
Fundraiser

The hospice is only part funded by the NHS. The challenge facing Sobell House is to raise over £1,500,000 per annum to maintain services. Apart from running costs the charity is fundraising to build a new unit to accommodate patients who are particularly frail and have complex conditions, plus an additional family suite where family members can stay overnight with the patient.

First of all I wanted to know how Lindsay came to work in this inspirational Headington institution.

"I was born and brought up in Denton near Manchester. After leaving school I went into the hospitality sector then later trained as a personnel manager.

After I got married I lived in Warrington and Chester but my husband Barry longed to travel and work abroad. We fulfilled his ambition and lived in Hong Kong from 1990–1992. By that time we had two children, Laura and Scott. Barry loved life in Hong Kong but it was hard for me bringing up two children aged 6 and 4 in a highrise apartment. When I became pregnant with our third child I wanted the birth to be in England. We returned to Cheshire but Barry was unable to find employment in the area. Soon after he found work in the South East and we moved to Oxford in 1994.

In 1998 I saw an advert for the post of hospice fundraiser and friends encouraged me to apply. Throughout my life I had gained experience organising events, not only in the hotel and leisure industry but in amateur fundraising too."

I wondered what was special about fundraising for the hospice. Lindsay said,

"Most of the people who get involved have a personal connection to Sobell House. They have experienced it through the loss of friends and family and have been touched by the experience. I have seen at close hand how getting involved with the fundraising helps people grieve. It turns a negative experience into something positive. They can run a marathon, take part in the Moonlight Walk, attend our Lights of Love memorial service or organise a fundraising event and do it in memory of their loved one. Often I work with people at an emotional time of their life and fundraising helps channel that emotion and can act like a therapy. My role is to support them with their fundraising, not only to achieve the best result for Sobell House, but also to help them cope with their loss. Also, as fundraisers, we raise awareness of the work done by the Hospice and all the services provided, and this is a key aspect of our jobs, so that the local community is aware of the importance of supporting Sobell House."

I asked Linday reflecting on her experience of Sobell House and what it could contribute to life on Oxtopia, to which she replied, "The importance of compassion and community."

Katy Hunt
Nurse Specialist

Oxford is a special place for Katy. Her mother Diane came to the city aged 15 and lived in a rented room in the top floor of a house on Folly Bridge. She worked in the millinery department of Elliston and Cavell Department store on George Street. Her father Anthony was an apprentice mechanic at Morris Motors in Cowley and proposed to Diane in the garden of St Mary the Virgin and Katy was born two years later in the kitchen of a tiny house on Woodstock Road.

Katy has lived in many counties in England but Oxford is the place she feels is home. She completed her nurse training here in 1990 at the John Radcliffe Hospital, living in the nurses' quarters of the Old Radcliffe on the Woodstock Road. After qualifying Katy worked on the surgical vascular ward at the John Radcliffe and enrolled part time at Westminster College to study for a counselling qualification. After a year nursing in Calcutta, Katy went to Durham University to study for a degree in philosophy and theology during which she continued nursing part time in Newcastle and even found time for some extra mural activities. Katy said, "It was there that I learned to row and three years later managed to compete for England, winning a gold medal!"

Katie was still only in her twenties and had a difficult decision to make. She said,

"When I considered whether or not to pursue a research-based career, I decided that I couldn't really do better than return to nursing. By that time I knew myself better and felt drawn to palliative care. I went to Bristol to read for a degree in district nursing."

After working as a District Nurse in Bristol, Surrey and Berkshire, stability came when Katy moved back to Oxford, got a job at Sobell House Hospice and enrolled at Oxford Brookes to study for the End of Life Care course.

Katy has worked at Sobell for fifteen years as a specialist nurse, a job which she is passionate about. "My role is to support people with a life-limiting illness in their last months of life. That involves thorough assessment of a person's physical, psychological and social wellbeing and identifying ways we can improve their quality of life, for example by achieving good pain control or by providing an opportunity to talk things through and plan for their future."

"I work in the Day Hospice. Patients who attend are all living at home and come in once a week for the day. I work with a team including Occupational Therapists, Physiotherapists, Art and Music therapists, a Chaplain and volunteers. It is a cheerful and safe environment where patients can enjoy a distraction from their illness whilst taking part in crafts or exercise classes, perhaps enjoy a jacuzzi bath if this is difficult for them to do at home and have access to skilled professional support and advice. Friendships are often forged amongst patients and also with volunteers. Patients say they value the sense of community and they feel well supported."

"My role in monitoring symptoms such as breathlessness or low mood is made easier because I am seeing the patients each week and can identify when there has been a change. I liaise with the patient's GPs and also with the medical team here at Sobell to treat problems as they arise to keep patients as comfortable as possible. A significant part of my role is providing psychological support at this distressing time and helping patients to identify what is important to them."

Katy's object that she will take to the dessert island is a candle. "We often light candles here to remember the still-present light of those who have died."

Chris Coutts
Social Worker and Facilitator

It is thanks to Welsh composer Edith Mary Harrhy (1893–1969) that a life enhancing Australian called Chris Coutts works at Sobell House. Chris's grandmother Edith met William Constant Beckx Daly while touring Australia and the couple married and later settled in Melbourne. Chris said,

"She influenced me a lot with her romantic tales of Europe and stories of the people she once knew like Noel Coward. She connected me to my British ancestry. In 2005 when I married Kayleen we were both up for adventure and thanks to my grandmother I have an 'ancestry' visa and can work here."

Chris's first degree from Queensland University was in Anthropology and that was followed by a degree in Social Work. Chris said,

"Anthropology is an essential part of my everyday work because it is the exploration of culture. How people think about death is cultural. But for culture to be positive it has to embrace change and my work involves trying to change culture. When I arrived in the UK I was shocked by how negatively social work and social workers are regarded. That is still a fact today unlike in Australia. Social work has a wider remit in Australia. One aspect of my work in Australia concerned Aboriginal land rights. In the UK social work jobs are mostly limited to Local Authority roles.

My first post in London was as a locum working on ways to save the council money. I found myself saying out loud 'I hate this job' and discovered that all my colleagues echoed my feeling. I looked for a more fulfilling post and started work at St George's Hospital Tooting and Trinity Hospice in Clapham Common. I worked with Professor Paddy Stone. He is a humble genius. When he appointed me, he asked if I had any questions. I asked him what he would like me to do and his reply was 'I have no idea.' I was the first social worker to be appointed to join his team. With a group of nurses I carved out a role."

In 2013 Chris came to Sobell House. Kayleen is a nurse and easily found work in the Churchill Hospital and he proudly told me that the previous week he watched her receive an award for outstanding nursing at the Town Hall.

Chris fulfils two roles at Sobell House: one is with fellow social worker Sabina Bi working with the patients and their families and the other is teaching and facilitating courses in the Sobell Study Centre. His specialisation is resilience and stress management which must help staff as well patients. He described his role with patients,

"My first remit is discharge planning. This may come as a surprise to readers but fifty per cent of the patients with life threatening illnesses once pain control and symptom management is in place can be discharged into the community and live much longer than they expected. We enable that by organising a package of care that can be delivered to their homes or arranging places in nursing homes.

The second role involves psychological/social care. You can regard death as a medical event with social consequences but I prefer to see it as a social event with medical consequences, like birth."

I interviewed Chris in a comfortable and calm room but he said it is not always like that.

"Social skills are needed. Birth and death are not neat. Expect rage, laughter and tears. The business of compassion has to be mixed with decision-making. Often people haven't thought through the financial consequences of end of life or issues like power of attorney and wills. Families don't always agree with care plans when it comes to patients who can be discharged. That is where a background in anthropology helps. I try to help people make a cultural adjustment."

Chris's desert island object was definitely Australian. It is furry toy wombat!

"He has come in useful on many occasions. A patient who was distressed and lonely told me she loved Australia. I fetched wombat from my office and she cuddled it .I let her take it away. The next time I saw her was on a chilly day and she was knitting the wombat a scarf. The week before she died she gave me the completed scarf."

Chris said that the philosophy he will take to Oxtopia is "A radical commitment to change. I have a deep regard for culture but it has to change to have life."

Dr Tim Harrison
Lead Clinical Consultant at Sobell House

In 1992 when Tim Harrison qualified as a doctor at St Georges Hospital, London, palliative medicine was not on his agenda. He embarked on a hospital career in gastroenterology. I wondered what happened to bring about such a radical change of direction. Tim said,

"An afternoon as a gastroenterologist could mean an endoscopy list of fifteen people. I would get to know what their bodies were like on the inside but I wouldn't get to know any of them as people. Palliative care is much more about the relationship with individual patients and that appealed to me. Having decided to switch, my first training post was at a hospice in Shrewsbury. I was fortunate that the senior consultant Jeremy Johnson was an inspiring person.

"I learned that although anyone can prescribe morphine, different prescribers will have different outcomes because the fundamentals of palliative care are about the individual patient and my relationship with that person. Palliative care is much more than the technology and the treatments alone."

In 2000 Tim Harrison went to Southampton where he worked with Professor Bee L Wee. She came to Oxford to head the Palliative Care Research Group which is based in the Sobell Study Centre. It provides leadership and administrative support for a programme of palliative care education, research and continuing professional development for health and social work professionals not only in Oxford but nationally and internationally. Tim said,

"In 2005, not long after she left Southampton I too came to Sobell House. Although Bee is still a consultant here she spends a lot of time in London as the National End of Life Care Lead spearheading the development of end of life care policy."

When I interviewed Tim he had not long succeeded Dr Mary Miller as Consultant and Clinical Lead at Sobell House. I asked him about his work.

"It involves a management role but my work is really about covering the in-patient unit seeing people who have advanced serious illness and whose life is coming to the end. Around 300 people each year spend their last days at Sobell House. We are taking a really challenging situation and making it slightly better. Patients come here with a life limiting disease and we look at the physical, psychological, social and spiritual aspects and how that affects them as individuals. We try to improve the quality of life for what is left of their lives.

At Sobell House we have a degree of knowledge and expertise and as people live longer we have to cater for increasingly complex medical needs. The important message is that hospices do a really good job but looking after people coming to the end of life should be for everyone including GPs and hospital specialists."

I asked Tim what he would take to Oxtopia from his experience of Sobell House.

"It is the importance of seeing everyone as an individual. It can be tempting to have an automatic process but every day at Sobell House we remind us ourselves that everyone is different in order to connect with each patient as an individual. The relationship between us is of one human being to another. We know it is bleak but satisfaction comes from making it less bleak."

Tim's inspirational item to take to the island was not far away.

"When Sobell House improved the entrance to the hospice, we commissioned a stained glass window. I'll take that both as a work of art and as a reminder of Sobell House.

Rev Bob Whorton
Chaplain

Bob was born in Lancashire in 1956 and brought up near the town of Basingstoke in Hampshire. Caring for people is at the heart of who he is. Bob said,

"At Sixth-form College I became concerned about people on the edge and began to volunteer at a centre for the severely disabled. I had a mystical experience which had me thinking about what life is about. It convinced me that I needed to serve but I didn't know how. I left school without the 'A' levels I hoped for and the consequence was experiences that influenced my path in life. In 1973, gap years were not on the radar. But that is what I had - a gap year which included working at a shelter for the homeless in Guildford. Most of the men had drug and alcohol problems. I was naïve believing I could help them. They were teaching me far more than I was helping them."

Being exposed to the complex and distressing lives of the homeless was a culture shock, even a trauma for the eighteen-year-old young man. Bob said,

"I felt dislocated and went to stay for a while in an open Christian community in Dorset called 'Othona'. It helped me to focus and I went on to study for a degree in social policy at Swansea University with my wife Sue (they met at Sixth-form College). We both wanted to be social workers and shared a desire to change the world!

"Instead of going on to social work training I got more involved in the church and began to train for the Methodist Ministry. During three years at a theological college in Birmingham our daughter Rachel was born. My first placement was to Dobwalls in East Cornwall. We were given a warm welcome by the chapels but there was some mistrust between the chapels and the community. I tried to break down barriers and build links between individuals and community groups. Our son Phillip was born in Cornwall.

"My next post was a complete contrast. I was sent to East Barnet in prosperous North London and worked there for seven years during which time I trained as a counsellor with the Westminster Pastoral Foundation."

After rural Cornwall and densely populated North London, his next appointment added to the variety and Bob, Sue and their family set off for the new town of Bracknell. As well as working in the district, Bob had his first experience as a chaplain: becoming a part-time chaplain at Broadmoor. After Bracknell the family moved to Basingstoke for two years where Bob was looking after two churches and working at Broadmoor part-time. Bob said of this "baptism of fire",

"It was exhausting and felt like juggling two full-time jobs. So I applied to Rampton High Security psychiatric hospital to become a full time chaplain. It was a fascinating time leading a multi-faith team and it taught me a great deal about mental health problems."

In 2006, having experienced human life in all its diversity, Bob became Chaplain at Sobell House. He says,

"In a hospice you are living with death every day. You are faced with your own mortality and the existential distress faced by people who are dying. It is a time of trauma for them and their families and Sobell is a container for that distress, for outpourings of anger and of love. It is a huge privilege to be with people when the depths of their being are touched. People's religious needs are different but spiritual care is the same for all – just being there. It is being there for the patients and their relatives but also for the staff."

At the time we talked Bob was about to become part-time at Sobell House. A new full-time chaplain joins him in 2017 to work for Sobell House and the hospital trust. Bob is planning to write including about hospital chaplaincy.

"My island object is a clay whistle in the shape of a bird. Its beautiful sound would remind me that chaplaincy is about listening to the song of the soul. Each person has a different soul and there is a depth of connection when people meet in distress .It is a soul to soul connection like the song of a bird."

Jonathan Punton
Volunteers' and Complementary Therapies Manager

Jonathan was born in Leamington Spa in 1981, but only because his mother just happened to be there at the time. His childhood was spent in a tiny hamlet called Sandford St Martin in the Oxfordshire Cotswolds. He said,

"Now I'm older I realise that it was an idyllic place. The verdant village of honey-coloured stone cottages and tiled roofs are beautiful but it has no shop or pub – its only communal building is a church. In the summer time I could roam free. I spent springtime on the nextdoor farm feeding lambs and learning to ride horses. My background is in sharp contrast to my upbringing. My English side is old school working class Northumbrian. My father Richard came from a fishing village called Newbiggin. I have moved around a lot and Northumberland is the closet place I can call home.

My father ran away aged seventeen to avoid being a fisherman or miner. After time spent in the Navy he became a chef. In the Navy my father learned boxing and passed a passion for the sport on to me. My mother comes from a wealthy family in South America so my identity can feel quite confusing, but I prefer it that way. After they married and had me my father, by then a successful chef,

commuted to Park Lane every day: a long commute but it meant we could live in our rural idyll.

"My mother Fazia was born in Wakenaam an island in the Caribbean which belongs to Guyana. She came to London with her parents in the 1960s after Guyana became independent and once in London my grandfather worked for the Bank of England. My mother is an artist."

After leaving school Jonathan went to Oxford College of Further Education to study journalism before embarking on a gap year. He said,

"I travelled and worked on a farm but spent nine months volunteering for small charities including a children's hospice in Guatemala. By the time I went to Goldsmiths to study Social Anthropology, I had acquired a taste for volunteering and the not-for-profit sector.

"Anthropology teaches you about people and cultures and when you learn about people you learn to respect them. That has had an effect on my career. While I was a student I volunteered as a youth worker and obtained qualifications in youth work.

Jonathan's first experience working professionally in a hospice was in St Christopher's South London which had been founded by Dame Cecily Saunders. He was appointed volunteers manager, but after living and working in London for fourteen years wanted a change of lifestyle and saw advertised a temporary post at Sobell House.

"Although a one year post was not what I had in mind, I love Oxford and knew that I could live in the country. I came here and am nearing the end of that year but I shall be staying on in a new role. The charity department and office and the clinical department and office are usually separate; my vision is to make those two worlds meet. I am fortunate because Help the Hospices has published a well-researched study titled 'Volunteering Vital to our Future' which supports this approach. Health and social care are under pressure. While we must not use a volunteer to replace a professional worker, the need for highly skilled volunteers to support them is growing. There will always be a need for the traditional volunteer as well. There are over 1000 volunteers involved with Sobell House: two hundred of them are involved in skilled face to face work and only seventy of them come in every week which is not enough to take on the future challenges we face in the sector. Skilled volunteers are not contractual. We invest time and money on training them. It is rare for a volunteer to let us down but it can happen. We do a lot of staff induction work and work to get the culture right at the start."

I asked Jonathan what happens when someone approaches him with an eye to volunteering.

"There is a long form to fill in which I help with and I usually ask 'Why are you volunteering?' There are many good reasons for volunteering. Some people want to volunteer for any local charity. Others, like retired nurses, want to use their skills and some people respond to a positive experience in the hospice wanting to give back. In my experience the only motive that doesn't bode well is when someone sees volunteering in a hospice as some kind of therapy.

Students make good volunteers. They are here for a shorter time but are full of energy are inquisitive and want to get involved. They are usually prepared to carry out tasks of a physical nature. Face to face work generally has the same shifts as the nurses. We are working with Brookes and the Oxford University Hub to try and make volunteering more flexible."

I asked Jonathan what he would take to Oxtopia and he showed me a photograph of Mohamed Ali which he keeps on his desk.

"I am passionate about boxing and Mohammed Ali is inspirational. He was strong willed, disciplined and determined. This job can be really hard and there are occasional moments when I feel like quitting; doing something else. On those days I look at this picture and it reminds me of the strength needed to carry on. It helps me to see the bigger picture and let the smaller things go, which is helpful both in work and in my personal life, He was a man who would put the greater good before his own personal gains, something I see in the best of our volunteers.''

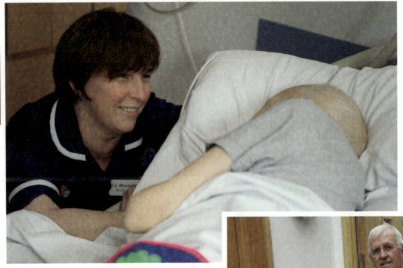

Castaway 3:1
Dwina Gibb

Dwina Gibb may not be as famous as her husband Robin Gibb, but then his band The Bee Gees sold more than 220 million records worldwide, making them one of the world's best-selling music artists of all time. But Like Robin, Dwina is creative and it was her artwork that brought them together. She is not only an artist but is also, a poet, author and dramatist.

The loss of her Robin in May 2012 is still raw for Dwina Gibb but the births of her first grandson Maxwell Robin two years ago and a second grandchild Theodore in 2016 have helped take the edge of her grief.

And there are other comforts too: Dwina told me a lovely story about how, while driving through a remote part of Rajasthan, she felt thirsty and pulled off at a small road side café which advertised a certain carbonated drink. (She thought that was a safer option than water.) As she walked in through the door she heard the sound of Robin singing *I Started a Joke*.

"Robin was singing to me in the middle of a vast desert. It was such a beautiful experience and I realised how their songs had reached every corner of the world.'

Creative In Her Own Right

Her first dramatic production *Last Confessions of Scallywag* played to sold out audiences at the Mill at Sonning for seven weeks in 2014. Sally Taylor, the director of the theatre, described it as 'Charley's Aunt meets Father Ted'.

Dwina's interests are varied. She is a collector of objects and sculpture related to mythology. She replaced an old tennis court in the grounds of her house in Thame, with a stone circle and in the centre has grown an oak tree from an acorn. The circle has been used for special marriage blessings, name giving and memorials. She is vegetarian and enjoys all religious or spiritual practices that encourage peace and happiness in the world, and particularly likes the yoga and meditation in the studies of the Brahma Kumaris. She is also the Patroness of the Order of Bards, Ovates and Druids. I wondered what strand of her life will determine what she chooses to take to Oxtopia and what was the origin of her creativity.

Dwina was born in County Tyrone in Northern Ireland – a place which has informed much of her life and is the origin of Dwina's dark humour and lively dialogue.

"I was brought up in the middle of the 'Troubles' and it felt like a war zone. I was aware of the darkness and the fear. My second school was the Collegiate Grammar School in Enniskillen. The school bus was diverted when a roadside bomb blew up a convoy of British soldiers and left a huge hole in the road. We never knew when there would be a bomb amongst civilians and, as a child, this was horrifying. My Uncle Ernie played the trombone in the local silver band and he expected to be with them at the November 1987 Remembrance Day Parade in Enniskillen. He was called away by the Bishop of Clogher who asked him to play *The Last Post* in his diocese so my uncle survived."

Ten civilians and a police officer were killed and 63 were injured in what has come to be known as The Poppy Day Massacre.

"A young girl who lived near us was injured and was in hospital for two years so the conflict felt close. Lots of people used wit and humour as a small light of hope. One of my choices for the island is George Frederick Watts' serene painting of Hope. She is depicted sitting on a globe, blindfolded, clutching a wooden lyre with only one string left intact."

Painting And Storytelling

Dwina said of her engineer father Edwin, "Dad bought me my first paint-box, and from that moment on, I painted portraits and sceneries. One of the first paintings I sold was of the racehorse Arkle. I loved drawing horses and swans. For many years I admired a painting of a swan on a mirror that hung in our home. I had never seen my father paint, but after our father's passing I discovered that the swan had been painted by him.

"My mother, Sarah Jane, who all her life has been called Sadie, was good at drawing, and she was the storyteller in the family. She made up wonderful stories for me and my sister, Thelma and my brother Raymond. Thelma and Raymond have stayed in County Tyrone. I'm the only one who had wings on my feet."

Dwina told me how a Catholic friend described to her the magical mythological stories of pre-Christian Ireland.

"I wanted to learn Irish so that I could read them. I asked my school if I could learn the language."

It was a sign of the times that instead of encouraging Dwina's interest they suspended her from school for a week accusing her of being 'subversive'. But Dwina knew what she wanted to do. "I wanted to be an artist."

She had begun entering art competitions as a child and won almost every one she entered. Her first exhibition was aged fourteen. But she didn't actually get to see it herself.

"It was in the town hall at Eccles and I couldn't afford to travel there. My aunt from Gloucester went to see it and sent me photographs. When Robin was the subject of 'Who do you think you are?' we went to Eccles Town Hall to research his great grandmother and great grandfather. I noticed some children's art work on the wall and realised that my paintings had once hung there."

The teenage Dwina was an admirer of Lindsay de Paul, the singer-songwriter and cartoonist.

"Lindsay had trained at Hornsey College of Art and I set my sights on studying there, too. After a working holiday in London, I knew that I wanted to leave Northern Ireland. But there was a problem. Northern Irish students were only allowed to apply to art colleges in England after being turned down by two in Northern Ireland. My art CV looked impressive and I took my A levels at 17 but I didn't want to go to Belfast School of Art," said Dwina.

"I deliberately made a portfolio of crude awful paintings. It was the hardest thing to do. The head of department who interviewed me saw on my record that I had won first prize for art in County Tyrone and he guessed what I was doing. I went red in the face but he turned a blind eye. Having achieved one rejection, I applied to Dublin. The application form arrived and it was all in Irish! Two rejections meant that I could apply to Hornsey where I showed my best work and was accepted. After Hornsey I studied textile design at Cat Hill in Cockfosters."

In the early seventies after Art College Dwina set up her own business in Shepherdess Walk, Islington. She designed and made children's bean bags and chairs in novelty shapes such as telephones, apples and pears.

"I sold them through *Time Out* but in my free time I was heavily into the Women's Movement, and campaigning for peace in Ireland. Most weekends I was on some kind of demonstration. I met the activist May Hobbs who had brought the night cleaners out on strike for equal pay in 1972. We went together to Manchester to support the women workers who were holding a Sit In for equal pay at a Small Parts Electrical Factory. Even their husbands didn't support their desire for equal pay for equal work. John Lennon sent a bunch of roses. May thanked him saying, 'Roses won't pay for the sit in'. He responded by sending her a cheque. Rowntree's and Cadbury's also gave the women financial support."

Enter Robin Stage Left

I asked Dwina how she met Robin.

"I hadn't seen my cousin Ken for a number of years. He came to see me in Plumstead where I was living at the time. He arrived in a Yellow Rolls Royce. I thought he must be doing rather well. But it was Robin's car and Ken was working as his bodyguard. Ken was interested in my work and after lunch I gave him some drawings. He happened to be on his way to the airport to pick up Robin who noticed the drawings and asked who had made them.

"Robin asked to see more of my work with a view to putting some of my paintings on the wall of the new house he intended to buy. Sarah Miles was a friend of mine and Robin wanted to meet her. I put them in touch with each other and they went out on a date. At Sarah's place he saw some more of my drawings. So it all came back to me again."

"At that time Robin was living with his twin brother Maurice because his marriage to Molly had ended. He asked to meet me with my portfolio to discuss a commission. We discovered that we had the same birthday: December 22. We also shared a similar sense of humour... A shared wit helped to sustain a long partnership."

"He thought I had a good artistic eye and asked me to help him view houses following his divorce. He was looking at London mansions but I thought it would be a miserable experience living alone in such large places. So instead I chose a little cottage for him in Barnes. At the time, I had no idea that it would become my home too. When I moved in with him, he carved our initials in a heart on the door post. He did that on every house we ever lived in."

Their son, Robin John (RJ) was born in 1983 and they looked for a larger house to accommodate him and Robin's children from his first marriage. In 1985 they moved to beautiful Prebendal House in Thame. Robin and Dwina married in Wheatley. Dwina said, 'When we arrived at the Register Office, the registrar had laid out a hundred chairs. She expected crowds. She looked disappointed when there was just Robin and I with Ken and his wife as witnesses. We wanted a very quiet occasion. We had even forgotten about rings and ended up giving each other the ancient rings we were wearing. We spent our honeymoon in Somerset staying in Wells and visiting Cheddar Gorge. We went to Wookey Hole – where there is a paper mill – and made headed notepaper for our house." I still have it.

A Woman In Love

Dwina may have been the inspiration for some of Robin's later lyrics. She said, "When I met him he was writing with Barry most of the songs for Barbara Streisand's album *Guilty*. He invited me to Miami. He was working on *I Am a Woman in Love*. One week I was working for him and the next I was a woman in love. That song has special meaning for me. We inspired each other."

We talked about Robin and Dwina's house in Miami where they famously hosted Tony and Cherie Blair and which they later sold. Dwina said,

"The house in Miami had quite a history. President Kennedy spent one of his last nights there before he was shot. Churchill painted there. Robin admired Churchill's daring. We've been inside Chequers. Another possibility for the island is the painting we saw there. It is by Frans Snyders on the Aesop Fable where the mouse frees the trapped lion by gnawing at the ropes. Churchill painted a rat over the little mouse. It was restored but a photograph of Winston's alteration is on display beside it. We have a photograph signed by Winston given to us by the photographer Christopher Barham."

I wondered how Dwina felt about Robin's adoring fans.

"You get used to it. I was never a jealous person and Robin's popularity meant that we travelled the world. Most fans were kind and loyal. The odd one gets obsessed or overcome with emotion. When we were living in Barnes, a young girl came down from Manchester and pitched a tent on our lawn. My cousin was able to track down her parents. She left behind her interior decorating books with instructions on how we should decorate our house. She had a very artistic eye, so I do hope she used that talent later. Some fans never marry but try to live your life. Their whole life is the adoration of the idol like virginal devotees. They all love the music and the sound of the voices and harmonies so much. I have seen and felt how the music touches the soul."

Irish Poets

The nearest occasion that Dwina had of becoming a fan herself was with the poet Seamus Heaney.

"In my twenties, I met him at a poetry workshop at the Yeats Society in Sligo. This was when he was less well known – before he received all the honours abroad. He said he loved my poem *Mullaghmore* [in Co. Sligo] and made me repeat it to the class. He particularly admired 'pinched hoof prints'. I noticed that no one had offered him a drink all day and I asked him if he would like a cup of coffee. 'You know', he said 'I'm dying of the dreuth.' I made him two cups and wrote a secret poem to him. I had observed him standing on a bridge in Sligo. I visualized him as: 'Pouring thoughts into a nameless river and I would gladly drink it dry.' The river was nameless because I couldn't remember which river flowed through Sligo. I slipped my poem under my own hand-made doily on an improvised tray, a biscuit tin lid, and presented it to him, then ran away."

Dwina made a delightful sketch of the future Nobel Prize winning poet and that is another of her possibilities for Oxtopia. She has a lifelong interest in Irish history and social politics and is also an admirer of the poetry of WB Yeats.

"I co-founded the Yeats Club which organises poetry competitions and published a journal called *Celtic Dawn*."

Celtic mythology has been the inspiration for her novels so far. *The Seers* and *Cormac: The King Making*. I asked whether that was the source of her spirituality.

"My Methodist grandmother was a big influence of me and she taught me to read the Bible and to pray. When I was eight I had an amazing vision of a tree of light with silver and gold leaves going back into the ground. It was as if I was being shown the cycle of life. I studied the *Tree of Life* in Qabalah and in Druidry and in ancient civilizations but I felt it was symbolic. I began to believe in reincarnation and became interested in aspects of Buddhism, early Christianity and Indian religions. I found out about yoga and meditation and I love the calm and contentment it gives me."

On one of her many trips to India, Dwina became involved in supporting out-reach programmes and water projects. She said,

"The strange thing is that when I came home I was thinking about water divining. When he was little RJ had talked about an underground well of water being here. We brought in a diviner and he proved RJ right. There is a fast flowing spring 200 feet below us and it could provide 600 gallons an hour. We know where it is should there be a drought here."

"An archaeologist friend took me on digs and gave me this cup found in Austria which dates from 600 BC. RJ showed me how it would have been used. He worked it out aged 6. That's another possibility for the island."

As well as her art, poetry and novels, another of Dwina's delights is Irish-inspired dialogue. In 2003 she created *The Gabby Aggies* a series of humorous dialogues between 'Mrs P' and 'Mabel' who provide a commentary on all kinds of events putting the world to rights. Following a performance on Manx Radio she was invited to do a one-woman show in New York.

We moved on to more tragic times. Robin's twin brother Maurice died in 2003 and Robin felt his loss deeply. He himself was diagnosed with cancer in 2011. While Robin was undergoing chemotherapy, Robin and RJ wrote the score for *The Titanic Requiem* to commemorate the 100th Anniversary of the sinking of the *Titanic*. Dwina said,

"If he had recovered Robin intended to go down to the sea bed to explore the wreck. *The Mozart Requiem* became Mozart's requiem and *The Titanic Requiem* was Robin's requiem. It was very special. He kept working and working on it with RJ right to the end."

Robin fell into a coma two days before he was due to attend the premiere. It took place on 10 April 2012 at the Central Hall, Westminster.

Dwina said, "We played all kinds of music to try and get him out of the coma. We played Bee Gees music but it was the *Confutatis* from *The Titanic Requiem* which brought him out. And gave us another three weeks with him. In his last days he wanted to watch comedies, Charlie Chaplin, The Marx Brothers, Norman Wisdom and Jack Black's *Gulliver's Travels*: anything comedic."

Robin died aged 62 in May 2012.

Dwina and her son lovingly put together the album *50 St Catherine's Drive* which contains Robin's last songs. Robin read Dwina's first play *Last Confessions of a Scallywag*, liked it and suggested making it into a film. After his death, it premiered in a small theatre in London. Uri Geller went to see it and his wife Hannah waxed lyrical about it to her friend Sally Turner and that is how it came to The Mill at Sonning for two months. For her next project Dwina would like to write about the Regency period and the Napoleonic Wars.

Dwina still lives in the thirteenth-century mansion which has been their home since 1985, and has spent the last two years designing and working with a stone mason, Martin Cook, on a grave stone for her husband. Dwina said "Robin loved roses and carried a stone from the tomb of St Cecilia, the patron saint of music." The symbolic stone is now in place.

I had to ask her that if she can only take one thing to the island what would it be? She said, "Robin's love was this house. He loved walking in the garden with his Irish wolfhounds. I don't suppose I can take the house and contents? "

I could see that it would be hard for her to leave behind all the works of art she has bought or made herself, the souvenirs of her travels with Robin, his awards for a lifetime in music and his musical instruments. We photographed her with an unusual Italian accordion. Dwina said "Robin used it to compose *I Gotta Get a Message to You*. It sits near Robin's brother Maurice's hat. If I can't take the house then I will need lots of paper and pencils so that I can write."

Dwina Gibb

Born: 1952

Occupation: Poet, artist and dramatist

Castaway Items: House, paper and pencils

Original OLE Interview: October 2015

For more information on *The Titanic Requiem* go to: www.robingibb.com

For more information about Dwina's books and plays go to: www.dwinagibb.co.uk

Aidan Meller

From childhood, a passion for art pulsed through Aidan Meller's veins but he didn't envisage that enthusiasm would lead to a career. When he eventually engaged with the public as an artist he realised he had discovered himself – and he could paint for a living. He is now a well-known art gallery owner in Oxford, and has become a promotor and patron of a new and exciting group of artists, The Oxfordians.

Aidan was born in Leicester. His mother, Christine was a teacher and his father Derek started a construction company. Aidan said, "I watched my parents work hard and struggle to improve their circumstances. Through their endeavours and their Protestant work ethic my father's business prospered. Having changed our circumstances, my parents sent me to a fee paying school, Dixie Grammar school in Market Bosworth. It felt like entering a different world. I was surrounded by wealthy people. I turned up in the family Ford car and they turned up in gold Rolls Royces. However the education was excellent."

"As a child I was bright but I've only really done one thing continually and that is Art. I have no other strings to my bow. I am fortunate as it is the most intriguing business. It involves fabulous people doing fabulous art. Art is about making connections and connecting to different worlds. And thanks to some help along the way, I have entered a completely different world from my childhood."

Aidan continued, "One of those influential people was my art teacher, Geoff Bailey. He was then a young teacher wanting to prove himself. We were fortunate – we had tiny classes, maybe five in the class. He was passionate beyond belief. He talked about Picasso as if he knew him. He breathed life into the great artists of the past and made it feel natural that we should be alongside these giants. He made me want to be an artist. Art pulled me along with the desire for a different life."

The long road to self-discovery

Aidan headed for Exeter University where he was taught art and art history by academics Leslie Cunliffe and Robin Mitchell. He said,

"Once again I found myself in another world. This existence was fully academic. I developed a love of art history. It felt like a hot bed of cross pollination through time. Exeter broadened my knowledge immensely."

I was surprised but interested by the subject of Aidan's thesis.

"I compared Joseph Wright of Derby with William Blake. It was a comparison of faith and reason of the mystic and the scientific."

Indian interlude

After university, Aidan's desire to get into another world transported him to another place but it also felt like travelling back in time. He went to a hill station in Tamil Nadu in India.

"I went to teach at the International School in Ooty. The style of teaching was of the fifties, it was mostly chalk and talk. The immediate environment with its language, cricket and afternoon tea felt like going back to another world. I lived in the west wing of an old Raj mansion with my own dhobi. I walked through botanical gardens to immerge into squalor, a parallel universe. I was a keen photographer. I photographed the contrasting and disturbing life around me. It was a moving and difficult time."

One encounter had a profound effect on Aidan.

"On one photographic expedition into the hills behind the school, I was completely on my own when I unknowingly alarmed a large buffalo. We both froze as we looked at each other in the eye. An idea overwhelmed me. I was over 5,000 miles from home and friends in an alien environment. What was I doing here?"

Aidan became ill with a serious form of gastroenteritis.

"I was wasting away and losing weight rapidly. The second time I went into hospital, I decided to go home. My mother met me at the airport and drove me straight to Leicester Royal Infirmary and I was admitted to the Tropical Disease Department."

"My body slowly repaired but my mind suffered. I wanted to do something with my life but I didn't know what to do. I thought I had left home for good and now I was back aged 22. I slid into a depression. Once I was physically strong enough I returned to Exeter and got a job as a teacher."

Aidan joined the staff of Sandford Peverell Primary School near Tiverton. He said,

"My father was cross with me and said 'I'm fed up of you telling me what you can't do. Tell me what you can do.' Because I was so low at the time, I felt I couldn't do anything, but it was helpful because it focussed my mind. I asked myself his question and realised that primary school teaching wasn't for me. I didn't think of retraining. I simply applied for a job at Henry Box School in Witney and got it." Once settled in Witney and in a happier frame of mind, Aidan returned to his father's question which had been nagging him.

I can paint

"'What can I do?' The answer eventually came...I can paint. So that is what I did. I painted. I noticed that people responded well to my paintings. I started to sell them and was surprised when they sold. I pondered on what to do with the money. In 1998, I went to the bank and in those bizarre days you could actually meet your bank manager. He still has no idea of the influence he had on me. As well as helping me set up a business account, he suggested that I display my paintings in the foyer." Aiden added, "To my surprise all the paintings sold."

This creative success gave Aidan the boost he needed to bring him out of his depression. He sought other outlets for his paintings.

"While still teaching, at the weekends, I exhibited at National Trust houses, at art fairs and other venues. Other artists noticed me selling well and asked me if I could sell their work too. I thought I was a good artist but I realised that I also had the ability to deal with people and introduce them to the world of art. I was still learning who I was when I started selling other artists work as well as my own. I had become a dealer."

It looked as if his career as an artist was threatened when Aidan was badly injured in a car crash.

"A German tourist was driving on the wrong side of the road when she collided with me. She had wandered in her mind back to Germany. The JR Hospital did an amazing job on my right hand. Every bone was broken. It took me three months to recover but the upside was that I received compensation and I used it to buy a printing press. After that I was able to sell prints of my work and of other artists."

At this point Aidan showed me one possibility for the island.

"I keep a note book for ideas and observations. I love these leather bound books with a flap for holding ephemera. I can't remember how many I have filled...an awful lot of them."

Art publisher

As Aidan published artwork his business started to grow in another direction and he reduced his teaching hours by going part time.

"I started my publishing business on the dining room table and with one employee as a sales person. We published art images in all their forms, posters, greetings cards, calendars, limited edition prints. When the business took off, I reduced my teaching to one day a week and employed two people. By the time I finished teaching, I had thirteen staff selling across the whole of the UK," Aiden continued.

"I decided to publish a catalogue of all the prints. Some companies give their catalogues away but I couldn't afford to do that. Even though I charged for them, all 2,500 sold. So I produced volume 2. From this emerged a publication which I called *Veritasse Magazine*.

"An American lady started to work for me at the time and she said 'There is nothing like this in the USA' and she was prepared to bet her job on the odds of it being a success in the States. I liked her confidence and we set off to pitch our wares at various trade fairs the USA. We sold and sold. It was the most spectacular trip of my life. We even sold calendars and posters to Wal-mart. That meant printing tens of thousands of them. At first we tried to print the orders ourselves but it was a logistical nightmare. We opted instead for selling the image rights. We were able to sell image rights to firms in South Africa, Australia and India as well as in the UK and USA.

"To sustain our success I decided to test the reaction of the public, face to face, by opening a gallery in Witney, on The Green in 2004. To my amazement it proved a success and soon the gallery was doing better by selling original paintings, than the publishing company selling prints. We moved from The Green to a more prime location on the High Street.

"Then I did something which has enabled me to specialise with confidence. I stumbled across Sotheby's." Aiden said. "Their executive business programme taught me how to navigate the art world. I was able to communicate with the top galleries in the world. I was incredibly privileged being able to question them. It was a formative experience and one that will have even more consequences in the future. I loved the years travelling to and from London."

Aidan's confidence had grown so when the shop next door became available he took on the lease and turned it into a café.

"The idea was that it would be an introduction to the gallery. But it was a disaster and I lost a huge amount of money. I had no choice but to close the restaurant and come up with a plan to cover the losses."

Art galleries

"I sold the publishing business and focused on the galleries (in 2006, I had opened our second gallery in Oxford, in Broad Street. It was great to have one focus. We now only sell top international artists. We also focused on rarer works, especially original works on paper."

The gallery in the Broad now specialised in Modernism. Aidan had the inspired idea of his gallery in The High specialising in the Pre-Raphaelites. Oxford can claim to have been at the heart of two art movements that influenced the world: the Pre-Raphaelites and the arts and crafts movement. The poster girl of the Pre-Raphaelites, Jane Burden was born in Bath Street off Holywell. Thomas and Martha Combe who ran the Clarendon Press and funded the building of St Barnabas Church were early patrons of the artists. They are buried in St Sepulchre's in Jericho. Then there's Holman Hunt's *Light of the World* in Keble College, Burne-Jones in Christchurch, Rossetti's Murals in the Oxford Union, and Millais' studio in the High... where better than Oxford to have a gallery devoted to the Pre-Raphaelites?"

Oxfordian art

Aidan's ambitions are growing. "I am interested in the whole cannon of art, the past, the present and the future."

Just as Oxford was at the heart of the Pre-Raphaelite movement, Aidan would like the city to provide the roots of a new art movement. He said,

"My interest in ideas of what makes art, have led me to work for several years with locally based contemporary artists who I would like to develop as a distinct group. For fun I'm calling them 'The Oxfordians'. My excitement is to get behind these contemporary artists. They will get my undivided attention as I display their work in the new gallery. After that I would like to launch them in London to the world."

Out of this long march of art, what would Aidan take to Oxtopia if he can only take one thing?

At this point Aidan pulled a small object out of his pocket. It was a rare half-crown. When Charles I and his army were based in Oxford, they needed money and so established a mint in the city. I'm sure many readers will be familiar with the Charles I Crown in the Ashmolean's coin collection. Aidan said, "They are very rare. Mine was given to me as a present. I learned that Charles had purloined the medieval silver from the colleges and melted it down to make coins. Holding this coin connects me to the history of our city."

"I must also take art and thinking about how my art teacher inspired me with tales of Picasso. The gallery has a rare portrait of Picasso's second wife Jacqueline Roque, which would remind me of the journey I have been on. It's a hard choice because I also love the gallery drawing by Chagall, of his love Bella. Both are really rare original works. I find that inside/outside world where artist use their personal life as a subject intriguing and attractive.

Aidan Meller

Born: 1973

Occupation: Art gallery owner

Castaway Items: Charles I Crown; Picasso's portait of Jacqueline Roque, and the drawing by Chagall, of his love Bella; leather bound books with flaps for holding ephemera

Original OLE Interview: May 2016

Annie Sloan

She is an entrepreneurial artist who from small beginnings and one shop in Headington has grown an international business with 1,700 (and counting) stockists worldwide. She is passionate about paint, a champion of colour and loud on the subject localism – and Annie promotes all three with equal and unstinting enthusiasm.

At a party in Montreal I was asked who I was going to interview next. When I replied, "You may not have heard of her. My next castaway is Annie Sloan", I was proved embarrassingly wrong. Annie Sloan shops aren't franchises selling identical products from identical premises. They are independent businesses with their own names and identities reflecting the location and the personality of the owner but trained by Annie Sloan to develop and express a certain Annie Sloan style. These outlets encourage the creative use of her specialist easy-to-use paints as well as stocking some of her 25 books and other products and running workshops in paint techniques for revitalising furniture.

Over the years this series has featured castaways from all walks of life and shown how people come to this international city from all over the world and thrive here. However, from my own experience, I know that for independent retailers, Oxford is not such fertile ground. The city has a reputation for being unsupportive of small retailers so I was particularly interested to find out how Annie's business with its flagship shop in the Cowley Road has thrived against the odds.

Annie said "My reason for settling in Oxford was its international nature. Almost everyone in my family was born in a different country. My father Charles Sloan was Scottish. My mother Dolores was from Fiji and I was born in Sydney, Australia in 1949.

"My father was a journalist and the family moved to the UK when I was ten. I can hardly count the number of schools I attended in different parts of the country before we settled in Kent where I went to school. My father's mother was from a farming background in Durham and Charles dreamt of being a farmer. He tried to fulfil that ambition in Kent. Despite his love of farming, he wasn't particularly good at it. He couldn't stop reading and writing so was something of an armchair farmer." Annie added.

"I loved him madly and he has been a huge influence on my life. I developed a passion for art and particular for paint early in my life. My father believed in me

and supported me. He introduced me to his artist friends and I knew at once that is what I wanted to be. I decided 'that is me'."

"I want something to remind me of my father on the island. That probably has to be this sculpture of a Roman head. It's only a replica made of a heavy concrete or something similar, so I painted it to give it more interest and light. I have it on my mantelpiece. It reminds me of home and my father too."

In the Mood

In 1966, Annie became a student at Croydon School of Art from where she went on to Reading University to study for an MA in fine art, spending altogether seven years in higher education. The art schools were breeding grounds for dynamic new concepts influencing life beyond the visual arts. Annie responded by becoming a member of a mostly girl band called The Moodies.

 "We were punk before punk", she said. "In those days most art students didn't wear makeup. It gave us a chance to dress up and give a highly visual performance. For one concert I wore a kangaroo costume made from brown chenille fake fur and appeared up a ladder throwing silver-foil-covered stars which I caught and put in the kangaroo pocket. Nowadays you might describe what we did as performance art. "

The Moodies were soon dazzling and appalling audiences from London to Berlin with gender-challenging cabaret routines. Where did their style come from? Annie said, "Marc Camille Chaimowicz [one of the first artists to merge performance and installation art] taught me at Croydon and made his class not just about life drawing. He opened it out into 'happenings'. Malcolm McLaren was also there as a student. In 1968/69, there were a lot of interesting things going on. Reading University was the meeting ground for Roxy Music and Brian Eno."

Annie added: "During the early 1970s, we attracted a cult following; Mick Jagger, David Bowie and Pink Floyd came to our performances. They liked our experimental unpolished improvisation and glam rock conceptualism. Pink Floyd asked us to be their backing group on an American tour but Roxy Music's first gig was supporting us," said Annie.

1974 was The Moodies most successful year but it was also their last. They were on the cover of *The Sunday Times Magazine* and a double page colour photograph depicts an unsmiling group of five young women and one young man, all of them wildly dressed and intensely made up. The young man was Rod Melvin their pianist.

Annie said, "The break up came when Rod Melvin was poached by Kilburn and the High-Roads and then by Ian Drury and the Blockheads. I loved being on stage and dressing up but I knew it wasn't really the life for me so I even turned down the chance to record for Chris Blackwell of Island Records. I took a part time job on Time Out as a theatre and music critic. I had no idea how lucky and privileged I was dropping into that job", see added.

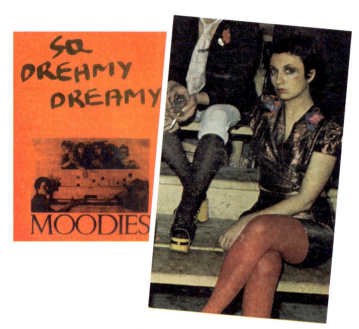

Left: Poster for The Moodies; Right: Annie as a member of the band in the Sunday Times

Bow to Battersea to Bladon

"But I really wanted to return to my first love – paint. In art school we had broadened our horizons with conceptual art but I wanted to take up the paintbrush again. I took commissions to paint murals for people. In the process I heard people talking about colour in a different way. Someone wanted their drawing room painted in the colour of mashed banana. I loved the idea of naming the tones and observing the subtleties of colour. I studied and observed the use of colour in later 18th century Sweden and that used by early settlers in the USA. Experiences in painting and decorating led me to think about it in a serious way. I learned that in 19th century Britain an apprenticeship in painting and decorating took seven years while to learn medicine it took just five years. I wanted to write a book about it."

In 1978, while Annie was living in Bow in East London in an artist's cooperative she was introduced to David Manuel. "He was acquainted with my room-mate and decided to call and see her. But she said 'I'm off to Paris.' So David and I spent the weekend together and that was it." Following a whirlwind romance they married in 1979 after which they moved to Battersea where their first son, Henry was born in 1981. Annie said,

"We moved to Oxford in 1982. David had read for his DPhil in philosophy here and loved the city. We both felt it would be a good environment for bringing up a family. Our first home was in Summertown where Felix was born in 1983. David was working in computing. We bought a house in Bladon in 1985 and David began to commute to London to work for Shell. After our third son Hugo was born in 1986, I felt the boys should see more of their father. I'd fallen into a conventional way of life and wasn't really enjoying it."

The quest for a unique paint and paint business

But Annie had taken her first steps into professional paint making in 1990. "I knew what I wanted and tried to find someone to make it in this country but without success. I discovered a firm in Belgium who were interested in the project. It took three months to-ing and fro-ing until we got it right. I liked Casein paints which are made from milk but chalk has a similar quality but is also able to absorb wax."

"Eventually we made twelve colours and two years later added a further twelve. We now manufacture thirty-two shades of my paint, Chalk Paint. I was the first to produce any paint like it – and many people have tried to copy it since – but I keep my formula secret."

The chance to change David's commuting life style came after the publication of Annie's first book. The Complete Book of Paint Techniques was written with Kate Gwynn and was published by Ebury Press in 1988. Its huge success selling hundreds of thousands of copies worldwide gave Annie and David a determination to develop their paint company.

"David left the job with Shell and instead took on short term projects while helping me grow the business. We organised our lives so that we both had plenty of time for the boys."

Annie explained that, at this time, they somewhat lacked confidence in their business expertise and sold the paint through a distributor. It went into a huge variety of outlets including specialist art shops and commercial paint shops. Experiencing the difference between impersonal outlets and smaller shops which specialised in interiors and decorating started Annie thinking about the philosophy of the business she wanted to lead. "We decided to start our own distribution company with the aim of selling only to independent businesses like our own. Our confidence grew as we realised that no one knew our business better than we did."

Since the success of that first book, Annie has produced a book every two years. She was thrilled to co-author her first book with her son Felix, a trained graphic designer who has worked in the family business from a young age, on Annie Sloan's Room Recipes for Colour and Style.

Running a local Oxford shop

Fifteen years ago she opened her first shop in Headington with Kathy Moss. "It was not long before it was just me. When I started running the shop I had no idea how difficult it would be. Big companies get lots of help and support but independent shops always seem to face obstacles. There are a few exceptional local authorities who understand the importance of diversity but most seem set on creating clone towns.

"At the moment the Cowley Road retains a unique character but the retail environment is being eroded. The Cowley Road should be protected as a location for independents but the pressure is on to make it just like everywhere else. I remember once going to a Gap Store in New York wanting to buy something that was an American statement only to discover that the stock was identical to that in their Oxford store. Why should anyone want to visit another English town to shop if it is exactly the same experience as on their doorstep?"

Visitors to the Headington shop began asking if they could set up a similar outlet. It was the age of the franchise but Annie had other more flexible ideas.

"People who like my style tend to be artistic and creative so don't want clone Annie Sloan, but they need a certain style. We learned how to support and train independent shops who want to sell our products. We began by supplying three shops and the three became twelve and then twenty and now it is 1,700 worldwide."

Running an international network of stockists

The international growth has been in the last four years. Annie said, "Before that we had experienced a difficult time. The mood at the millennium was to throw out the old, have a clean sweep and want everything new. The big opportunity for us came after the financial crash. In 2008, people felt they couldn't move house and couldn't afford to spend a lot of money on furniture. By that time, the internet had become the forum it is today. People came across my ideas for painting furniture and creating a new look in a way that was quick and easy. They learned that my paints can be used on un-primed un-sanded surfaces and on almost any material from wood to metal and plastic." Annie added "And my brushes make applying it quick and easy. Instead of buying an expensive new kitchen they realised they could paint their old one with style."

"Ireland was our first success story outside of England and that was followed by the USA, the rest of Europe, Canada, Australia, New Zealand and South Africa. Our latest entry is into Japan. I am really proud of how our business has grown organically," Annie said.

"We encourage the shops we supply to adapt to their premises but they all have an interior decorating feel to them. One of our stockists is in Marlow is called Home Barn. It is in a barn which has the space for Country and urban vintage pieces. Another stockists of mine is Piorra Maison in Montreal – this shop is very 'warehouse chic'."

"Independent shop keepers have the knowledge and enthusiasm to discuss with their customers how they can achieve what they want in their homes. Most of the businesses we supply are family businesses, often started by women, but as they become successful they are joined by husbands, sons or daughters – nearly all are family affairs as is our own. Felix is now our branding director and his partner Lizzy our marketing manager."

Not everyone in the family is involved. Henry is a primary school teacher and Hugo is a musician otherwise known as Chad Valley. The firm now inhabits a huge warehouse near the BMW factory yet manages to maintain a 'homely' feel through judicious decorative and furniture painting.

Annie is now a regular jet setter travelling the world promoting her brand, appearing on TV and radio (she was on Radio 4's Woman's Hour recently) and a fan of new media. So how would she feel being confined to our desert island? Admittedly Oxtopia now has a population of nudging 100 so it won't be solitary confinement. What will she be taking with her if it can only be one thing?

"Castaway objects – I have so many beautiful and interesting paintings I would want to take, usually discovered in auctions, car boots and junk shops. My house is stuffed with them but my final choice is the fake Roman sculpture."

Annie Sloan

Born: 1949

Occupation: Artist and paint entrepreneur

Castaway Item: Sculpture of a Roman head

Original OLE Interview: August 2014

Castaway 3:4 (and 1:1)

Christopher Brown

Professor Christopher Brown CBE, the three hundred and thirtieth director of the western world's first public museum, the Ashmolean, was our first castaway when this long-running series began. On his retirement – and on receiving the freedom of the city – we revisit the life and times of the man who has overseen a wonderful sixteen-year transformation of the University of Oxford's museum of art and archaeology.

Since its opening in 1683 (originally located in the Museum of The History of Science in Broad St) the University of Oxford's museum of art and archaeology has been a rare place where town and gown meet. However, a member of the public visiting before Christopher arrived on the scene in 1998 would have had a very different and less welcoming experience than he does today. The visitor now enters an inviting space where the Rick Mather-designed stairway beckons us towards a journey in time and place.

It is not just the new building which Christopher has overseen but also the revitalising of the education department, the links with schools and the rearrangement of the collections on the theme of Crossing Cultures Crossing Time – a theme which fits perfectly with the museum's open access policy connecting the university to the town and county, the country and the world. The physical changes are there for everyone to see but the change in culture, while not tactile, is every bit as real. That is why, under his stewardship, visitor numbers have risen from 200,000 to close to one million.

Gibraltar and Tangier

"My grandfather was a miner and my father, Arthur, left school aged 14. He had a flare for technical drawing and, instead of going down the mine, became a trainee draughtsman in an asbestos factory – an environment which gave him an opportunity but would eventually cost him his life. He died of mesothelioma in 1991. Shortly before the war he joined the Auxiliary Air Force and, at weekends, learned to fly. He was one of the first to be called up in 1939. He flew Spitfires and was fortunate to survive the Battle of Britain. Like many ex-RAF pilots after he was de-mobbed he started a career in commercial aviation. He began working for Gibraltar Airways and flew Rapides, bi-planes with a handful of passengers, between Gibraltar and Tangier. My parents spent six months of the year in the Rock Hotel in Gibraltar and six months in Tangier ".

Christopher continued: "A few years ago, my mother, Marjorie (in her mid-nineties and living in Bloxham) and I took a trip to Tangier: we found the nursing home where I was born. When I was being a difficult teenager, my father would jokingly threaten to alert the Moroccan Embassy to have me conscripted into their military service."

Late in 1948 the family returned to the UK and his father went to work for British European Airways, now BA.

"My father flew for BEA out of Heathrow so we settled at Ickenham near Uxbridge. I began at the local primary school but my secondary education was as a dayboy at Merchant Taylors' School."

"We had an enthusiastic art teacher who encouraged us to visit the Goya exhibition at the Royal Academy in 1964. I became obsessed by Goya as a printmaker and that prompted my first ever art lecture – to my fellow sixth formers. To this day I have a profound love of the work of Goya. I remember only one art book at home, on the Group of Seven." In the early 20th century The Group of Seven tried to create a truly Canadian artistic tradition. "On a recent trip to Canada, I saw some of their work and the memories came flooding back,"

Building blocks to a museum career

"At the age of sixteen, having visited Knossos and pursuing an interest in Minoan archaeology, a school friend and I got on our bikes and cycled down the A40 to Oxford and stayed at the Youth Hostel which, as I remember, was then in Headington, in order to visit the Ashmolean for the first time."

"Had I known about art history at the Courtauld that would probably have been my first choice for University. However, I was persuaded by my teachers to apply for either archaeology at Cambridge or history at Oxford. I had been treasurer of the Archaeological Society at school which had produced well-known archaeologists like Martin Biddle. In the event I applied to St Catherine's at Oxford and was accepted to read history."

I asked Christopher if the college's striking modern architecture by Arne Jacobsen had influenced him.

"I was in Copenhagen earlier this year and saw the remarkable SAS building again. It was Jacobsen's Aarhus City Hall that convinced the first master of the college, Alan Bullock, to choose him. I do think St Catherine's is a great building. It has certainly influenced my attitude to contemporary architecture. When it came to the building of the new Ashmolean, I wanted a contemporary building and not a pastiche of nineteenth-century architecture."

While a student at Oxford, Christopher met his future wife Sally, the daughter of a don at Brasenose. She is two years younger than him and read English at Somerville. He said,

"Sally got a first and I got a second, a fact that she has frequently brought up in the course of our married life! We married in 1975 and shortly afterwards she became a curator of literary manuscripts at the British Library. She looked after manuscripts from Keats to Pinter until her retirement in 2008."

At the National Gallery – a 27-year stint

"I had done the postgraduate Diploma in the History of Art at Oxford. My tutor was a remarkable man – a great Belgian scholar, Bob Delaisse, who was a Fellow of All Souls. I was enormously impressed by his knowledge and his enthusiasm and took the course he offered on early Netherlandish painting. If anyone has to take the blame for my career as an art historian, then that person is Bob Delaisse."

"I had just registered for a DPhil with Bob when the previous curator of Dutch and Flemish painting left the National Gallery. I applied for the job and despite my modest knowledge of the subject, I was appointed. In those days there was a very different attitude. People were often hired on their promise rather than their achievement. I stayed for twenty-seven years."

"While I was working at the National Gallery I was given some time off to do a PhD at the Courtauld Institute on the subject of Carel Fabritius, Rembrandt's greatest pupil. My distinguished supervisor was Michael Kitson. The artist he loved above all others was Claude. I was delighted when he made a heroic effort to come to the Ashmolean in 1998 to see an exhibition of drawings by the artist. By then he was seriously ill and he died soon after but he was proud that a student of his was Director here."

"At that time I also became very interested in the social history of art, the way that art works in society and the functions it serves. The modern art market was born in the seventeenth-century Dutch Republic. There were exhibitions and dealers and auctions, all the features of the modern art market.

Christopher's life at the National Gallery was an excellent preparation for what was to come at the Ashmolean. He explained,

"In 1971 the Gallery was opening up to a broader public. Michael Levey became Director in 1974. I admired him very much indeed. He created an ambitious education department and mounted the first substantial exhibitions. His aim was to open up the museum in the way we now expect of museums. That is where and how I learned to do it: annual visitor numbers at the National Gallery have grown since the early 1970s from half a million to six million today."

"I was also involved in the two large building projects: the first being the Sainsbury wing. A competition was held in 1981 to choose the architect to build it.

"When Michael left in 1986, Neil MacGregor became Director. We worked closely and successfully together. We are different personalities but we shared the same vision and ideas about what a museum could and should do.

"During those twenty-seven years I was very happy and never applied for another job. I left a lot of my heart in Trafalgar Square when I moved to the Ashmolean in 1998."

A new vision for the Ashmolean

At the selection interview for the directorship of the Ashmolean, Christopher made it clear that if he were appointed he intended to open up the museum to the community at large.

"I told the panel that if that was not what they wanted they shouldn't appoint me. I believed this new public face would involve a new building."

The Ashmolean's collections are a national treasure, comparable to the very best in Europe, but in 1998 many artefacts were poorly displayed. New temporary exhibition galleries were needed too.

"While in London I had worked with Lord Sainsbury at the Dulwich Picture Gallery as well as at the National Gallery. I asked him if he would help me to transform the museum. I was also very fortunate that Sir Ewen Fergusson, the former Ambassador to Paris, gave a generous gift - enough to allow me to commission a masterplan for the future of the building. I admired what Rick Mather had achieved at Dulwich and so in 1999 I asked him to produce a masterplan for the Ashmolean. We then organized a formal architectural competition and, although many architects from around the world applied, Rick was appointed.

"Then we needed to raise the money – £70 million for the two stages of the project. John Sainsbury committed to make a large donation at an early stage and together with university support that helped us win a Heritage Lottery grant of £15 million. That moment in 2004 was wonderful. It was the moment when the dream became reality. We knew then that it was going to happen."

Turning a dream into reality

Leading the rebuilding project was an enormous undertaking but ensuring the support of the staff and changing the culture within the museum was the most difficult part admitted Christopher.

"There have been museums where an incoming Director with new ideas came up against an entrenched and resistant curatorial culture. And that can be very painful. I didn't want that to happen here. What I felt I needed to do was to take time to consult everyone. It was a long process in which everyone's view was sought and taken into account. Many, many meetings took place and colleagues came to accept the need for change."

On display at the opening of the new Ashmolean in 2009 were artist in residence Weimin He's visual story of the rebuild. What struck me at the time was how Christopher had created an inclusive environment. There were the security staff, the electricians, secretaries, volunteers as well as the academics, the builders and the architect and they all came from different backgrounds and ethnicities. I thought that Christopher could teach a lesson in successful management.

Then there was the reorganisation of the collections.

Christopher said, "Departmental display must inevitably stress cultural difference: here is European art and there, in another part of the building, Asian art. It puts cultures in hermetically sealed boxes. The idea of *Crossing Cultures Crossing Time* is to emphasise cultural exchange. That is how civilisations really work."

Displaying paintings is relatively easy compared to the problems of displaying the kind of archaeological material held by the Ashmolean.

"I had no clear idea of how to do it." Christopher added, "the idea of the new display strategy really did grow out of the discussions inside the museum and within the wider University which began in 2000 and lasted until 2007."

Lovers of the Ashmolean have reason to be grateful for Christopher's patience and vision. When I interviewed him back in 2007, Christopher focused on the 'Treasures' Gallery for his island objects. At that time the demolition of the old galleries was underway and he wanted to keep the rest of the museum as inviting as possible in the circumstances. His choice then was the Alfred Jewel.

He is embarking on four years as a Research Professor in preparation for an exhibition provisionally entitled Rembrandt's Leiden in collaboration with the Lakenhal Museum in Leiden. Twinned with Oxford, Leiden is Rembrandt's birthplace and scene of his early triumphs.

Christopher said, "In addition I will work on Anthony van Dyck's stay in Italy and on the social history of Dutch art. The early years of the Dutch Republic is the perfect time and place to examine the social function of art."

"So while I have the Alfred Jewel to remind me of Oxfordshire, this time I'd like to take with me Rembrandt's deeply moving drawing of his father. It was made shortly before his father's death in 1630 and is inscribed prominently by Rembrandt with his father's name. Drawn in red and black chalks with a brown wash, it is testimony of great love and compassion."

Christopher Brown

Born: 1948

Occupation: Past Director of the Ashmolean Museum, Oxford

Castaway Item: Rembrandt's drawing of his father

Original OLE Interview: September 2014

Castaway 3:5
Icolyn Smith

In her mid eighties, Icolyn Smith still feeds the homeless from her so called 'Soup Kitchen' in the Asian Cultural Centre on the Cowley Road. So called because although she does make delicious soups, the roast dinners she serves there could grace The Ivy or The Randolph. She remains a remarkable woman who inspires everyone she meets.

Empathy drove her to start the soup kitchen twenty-six years ago and she still has it in bucketfulls. She says, "My heart goes out to young mothers I see trying to cope. They remind me of myself when I had three jobs, leaving the house without breakfast early in the morning, grabbing a slice of toast to eat on my way to work."

Food of one kind or another runs through her story and the most interesting food stories come from the place of her birth, Coolshade in Jamaica.

From Coolshade to Cowley Road

Coolshade is only twenty miles from the bustle of Kingston but as Andrew Bax, who published her biography, says, "In the 1930s, when her story began it was a rural self-sufficient community of scattered single storey timber houses with wattle walls and roofs made from thatch or corrugated iron."

Icolyn told me about her first day at school. "I was aged seven and my older sister took me on the long walk to school. I was so small that the teacher picked me up and sat me down at the front of the class."

Icolyn had five brothers and four sisters and they all worked on the smallholding before leaving for school.

"My work was to pick up the eggs. We fed the chicken with corn every morning but then they scattered into the Blue Mountains. They roosted on bamboo – like steps near the house and the rooster would wake us up early in the morning. They laid their eggs among the pineapples so it was not easy collecting them without being scratched by the pineapple prickles. My next job was to collect water from the springs between the rocks. We stored it in clay pots with lids which kept it icy cold.

We had to be at school for 9am or we were in trouble: that often meant running there to avoid losing our playtime. Teachers were well respected."

Icolyn does not look her age and she has the energy of a much younger woman.

She said, "All the fresh and natural food we ate as children has made us healthy. We grew our own coffee, cocoa beans, peas, beans, yam and sweet potato. We kept goats, pigs and cattle and all of them thrived on the lush vegetation. We grew rice in the lower streams among the rocks but it involved a lot of work for a little rice."

Given her reputation as a chef, I wondered when she learned to cook.

"My mother taught me when I was six or seven. Everything we ate was freshly picked and freshly cooked and delicious. I taught my daughters to cook and they can all improvise and produce a healthy meal from a few good ingredients. A lot of young mothers in Cowley have not been taught and don't really know how to cook. I can make a good meal for five to ten people for £5."

Icolyn was a bright girl but her education was cut short when she was needed to help with the child care of her sister's child Monica and a younger sibling, Enid. She left Coolshade to live with her sister Mary in Kingston when she was eighteen.

Icolyn said "I was young and loved the bright lights and the music and dancing. The music was not electronic but with saxophones, guitars and drums. But what shocked me greatly was that I had to buy food, especially fruit. I was used to picking it off the trees and now I had to use my hard earned money to buy it."

Icolyn married Eric Smith in 1953 and the whole neighbourhood celebrated into the small hours of the morning. Life was tough but Eric and Icolyn worked hard, he as a carpenter and she in domestic service. They were eventually able to buy a two bedroom bungalow in Waterhouse where they brought up four children, Norman, George, Pamela and Paulette. Kingston became an edgy and dangerous place to live in the sixties. In 1966, Icolyn's brother Colin worked as a barber in Kingston and was attacked for no reason on his way home and died of the stab wounds.

But when that happened Icolyn and Eric were 4,500 miles away in Oxford. They had become concerned for the future of their children. Eric came here first by sea and started off with his sister Gertrude in London. In 1960, he responded to a call for skilled workers at the new Atomic Energy Establishment at Harwell and that is how he came to settle in Oxford. When, in 1965, he sent for Icolyn she flew here and their first rented home was in Chilswell Road , South Oxford. The children were sent to Coolshade with their grandparents until the Smiths could raise the money for their fares. I asked Icolyn about her first impressions of England.

The immigration trail

"As I looked at all the grey buildings in London; most were belching smoke. I asked Eric if they were factories because of the chimneys. He said 'No they are houses.' In Jamaica the only buildings which had chimneys were factories."

Icolyn wasted no time in finding a job. Two days later she was working in the canteen at the British Leyland car factory in Cowley. Icolyn said,

"It was April and I remember the time exactly: it was 2pm when I looked out of the canteen window to see this white stuff falling. 'What is it?' I asked. 'Snow' was the reply. 'Can you walk in it?' I enquired. But when I walked in it I didn't like it at all. There was ice everywhere. And it was cold. In those days we warmed our home with paraffin heaters."

Icolyn and Eric's story follows a familiar pattern of immigration in those days. They worked industriously and were able to put down a deposit on a house in Randolf Street off the Cowley Road. It was to this house that they brought their four children. The children had to travel unaccompanied due to the high cost of airfares relative to average income in those days. Icolyn and Eric grew anxious when the flight was delayed. As soon as they arrived at the terminal, their parents bundled their children into unfamiliar coats and other warm clothes.

Number 35 became their home for the next twenty-one years. Their spirit of generosity meant that the once spacious house overflowed. Icolyn began working as a home help. She said, "I got the impression that people didn't care for other people."

That certainly wasn't the case at number 35. In that household shelter – and the cooking pot – was extended to anyone in need, of any race or background.

Norman asked his mother if he could bring home a school friend for lunch. His friend Hilroy Burton was from Antiqua. Hilroy's home circumstances were unstable and regular lunches at Randolf Street extended until he moved in and lived with the Smiths. Icolyn rescued a hungry family from a damp ridden house nearby. They stayed with her until they were able to find suitable accommodation. That is just a sample of the welcome at number 35.

Dealing with discrimination

Icolyn said that because of discrimination life had not been easy for her children "When they joined East Oxford School they were among only seven black children so there was a lot of name calling."

It is hard to believe the reaction of one mother. Icolyn snatched a boy from the path of a fast approaching car in the Cowley Road only to be told by his mother 'take your black hands off my boy.'

Discrimination became a big problem for Norman. He was taken on as an apprentice electrician by local contractors Ilco. Under the arrangement he was meant to be given a day off to attend the College of Further Education like all the other apprentices. The white apprentices did indeed attend college and so got their qualifications, but Norman was kept back and made to work every day. It is good that Icolyn's grandchildren will not have memories of the Cowley Road barber who would not cut black people's hair and of shop assistants who did nothing to hide their dislike of serving a black person.

Among Icolyn's happiest memories is the time starting in 1970 when she worked as a nurse at Cowley Road Hospital. She trained on the job under the watchful eye of Staff Nurse Holywell. Much of that happiness was due to the appreciation of the patients who enjoyed her sense of humour and encouragement. Tragedy struck in 1975 when Eric became ill with a malignant tumour. Icolyn cared for Eric at home until his death in March 1976.

It was after this that Icolyn often juggled three jobs to make ends meet. Eric and Icolyn's youngest son Gary had been born in Oxford and was still in primary school and her daughters were teenagers. She wanted to be at home for them at the end of the school day. So she applied to Oxford Social Services to become a care worker. That is the job she did for the next twenty-four years. Icolyn said "I liked my elderly clients and built up strong relationships with them but care workers are not valued by their employers."

That becomes obvious in the next part of Icolyn's story which is about the origin of the Oxford Community Soup Kitchen.

Oxford Community Soup Kitchen

"One of my clients was Bishop George Appleton who lived in James Street. I finished work there at 6.30pm and was on my way to see my next client when I noticed a young man scavenging for food in concrete refuse bin. I was so shocked that I stopped and prayed 'Something has to be done, Lord. What can I do?' It was like a vision: the sunlight appeared brighter. I knew I had to do something."

What Icolyn did was to talk to her family and her church, The Church of God of Prophesy. She told them that she wanted to open a soup kitchen but had nowhere to do it and no money to fund it. Good news came from The Asian Cultural Centre. The manager Jawaid Malik said the Asian dressmakers no longer needed it on Wednesdays so she could use it for her soup kitchen. Her first attempts at securing a grant failed but after the Bishop gave a donation, then Tyndal House rang to say they had £1,500 unspent budget which she could use. The church members rallied round as volunteers and so the kitchen was soon up and running.

Icolyn said "Andy the manager of Alders butchers offered fresh bones for boiling up as soup. I added vegetables and spices and a healthy soup has featured as a starter ever since. To begin with we had to use our own pots."

Mr Malik kept the rent as low as possible and put notices in pubs, shops and hospitals and offers of help came in. The reason it had to be on a Wednesday was because Icolyn had contacted her supervisor and asked if she could reschedule her Wednesday clients so that she could have the day off to run the soup kitchen. They agreed to the day off but it was without pay. The Soup Kitchen opened on 28 of September 1989. Icolyn said,

"On the first day nine men came along including the tattooed young man who I had seen scavenging. Anticipating more the next week, I bought two sacks of potatoes. Word got around and sixty people came."

Most of them were white men who had been overcome by financial and marital problems and others had sunk under the influence of drink and drugs. Most of them had lost all hope and self-respect and they stank. Icolyn said,

"I wondered what to do about it. I encouraged them to use the centre's wash hand basins, to discard their old clothes and put on ones from the second hand clothes we collected. Sometimes it only takes a clean body in clean clothes to make a man without hope feel better."

Icolyn gave them something most had not experienced for a long time; touch. She told me the story of Charlie.

"When I met Charlie he was young but you would think he was old. No shop in the Cowley Road would let him into their shops. He came to the Soup Kitchen and stood on the threshold his arms folded and his eyes glaring in an aggressive and angry pose. I went over to him and put a hand on his shoulder and said 'It's alright son.' He started to cry. I gave him a hug and he looked at me and said 'Will you be my Mum?' That's all he needed...to feel a loving touch. Gradually he started to put his life in order and began to help in the kitchen. He got a place to study at Ruskin College and started to work at the Probation Centre to help young men who had got themselves into similar situations. He thanked me and said 'Ma, no one but you could get the Charlie out of me.'"

That is just one story of one of the lives Icolyn has turned around. Her generosity was recognised on 13 November 1998 when her name was on the New Year's honours list.

Since then Icolyn became something of media star when, in November 2011, the Soup Kitchen was used as a venue for Channel 4's Secret Millionaire. She thought they were filming a programme called Food for Thought. Successful restaurant owner Arfan Razak was the secret millionaire. He admitted to Icolyn that he was likely to turn aside from homeless people thinking they might mug him. Icolyn took him to task. "You have no right to judge anyone. It could be you."

By this time Icolyn had moved to Kelburne Road and on the last day when, abandoning his assumed name, Raz went to give her a cheque, he held her hand tightly. She asked why. He said "Because I've been lying to you and I'm afraid you might hit me."

When she thanked him for his cheque she said, "The love of people is the best riches you will ever have. Live for others – life is for sharing."

"Live for others – life is for sharing."

That is what Icolyn has done all her life providing a wonderful example to all of us of how to live a good life. As Raz said "Ma Smith is one in a million." She used his cheque to open the kitchen on Saturdays as well as Wednesdays..

It feels unkind to tear her away from her vibrant extended family to send her to Oxtopia. She said, "I must have my photograph albums and that way take my family with me and I can't be without my Bible."

I asked her if there was anything else she would like to take? I promised her that there is a copy of all the major Holy Books on the island.

"Can I take my watercolours? I love painting and maybe I'll take a painting of the colleges to remind me of Oxford."

Icolyn is a big supporter of the Cowley Road Carnival. In 2014 she was a proud mum when Gary performed under his professional name DJG. Although 83 at the time, Icolyn was up at 6am getting food ready for her stall.

Icolyn Smith

Born: 1935

Occupation: Soup kitchen lady

Castaway Item: her photograph, Bible, painting of Oxford colleges

Original OLE Interview: August 2015

From Coolshade to Cowley Road by Andrew Bax is published by Bombus Books (£7.99) – all proceeds are being donated to the Icolyn Smith Foundation.

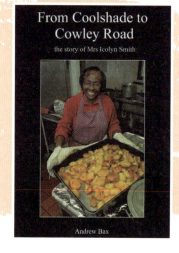

From Coolshade to Cowley Road
the story of Mrs Icolyn Smith

Andrew Bax

Castaway 3:6
Estelle Bailey

Chief Executive of the Berkshire, Buckinghamshire and Oxfordshire Wildlife Trust (BBOWT), Estelle Bailey is driven by a desire to save our landscape and wildlife.

A quick scan of BBOWT in numbers reveals what an impressive organisation it has become in the last fifty-five years. It looks after ninety nature reserves covering 2,524 hectares, three Living Landscape schemes covering 123 sq. km. It has 52,000 members and has a small 'army' of 1,410 volunteers. That an organisation like BBOWT is badly needed can be understood by another statistic: 97% of wildflower meadows were lost in the previous century.

The outdoor life has been important to Estelle Bailey since she was a child, and her personality and her way of life are bound together in her passion for nature.

Estelle believes "Nature is fading away" and that Oxfordshire in particular needs robust protection because it is threatened by further urban growth. Estelle wants BBOWT to work with developers to fulfil the need for housing but also to create and preserve natural space for wildlife which she believes is also needed for healthy human life.

Linking up nature sites

In her role as Chief Executive she has worked to bring organisations like the RSPB, the National Trust, Oxford Preservation Trust and Earth Trust to join forces to take a strategic landscape scale approach to conservation. Estelle says, "Linking up fragmented sites across the river valleys of the Upper Thames will enable more wild life including rare plants, insects, birds and mammals to thrive and survive as well as providing essential services to people like flood attenuation."

One of those rare plants, the snake's head fritillary, regarded as the symbolic plant of Oxfordshire, shows what a difference BBOWT can make for wildlife.

"We've been managing Oxford City Council's Iffley Meadows nature reserve since 1983. Each year the grazing regime and overall management has improved the conditions for the snake's head fritillaries. In April we recorded a record-breaking 89,830 snake's head fritillary plants flourishing in this important reserve beside the River Thames," said Estelle.

Estelle is well qualified to oversee BBOWT's new five year Strategic Plan, launched in 2016 because, in 2007, she directed a pioneering project called the Pumlumon

(pronounced Plynlimon) Project in Mid-Wales. It covered 150 square miles and used a method which helped farmers, tourism businesses, foresters and water companies manage land differently so the whole upland landscape could revitalise. Bogs were brought back to life holding water and storing carbon again, grazing patterns changed, cattle were reintroduced and trees planted, and at the same time, wildlife tourism flourished. This once-barren upland landscape in Mid-Wales came back to life. "We were pioneering an upland economy built around wildlife, ecology and long term sustainability. We helped local communities keep farming, earning a living, just by doing things a bit differently. It was a new way of working, with nature, rather than against it." The Pumlumon Project has become a beacon for similar projects all over Europe.

Grass roots

But when and where did her love of nature begin?

"The first seven years of my life were spent in Cannock in Staffordshire. When I was eight, we – my Mum and Dad and my sisters Joanne (now 46) and Georgina (now 37) – all moved to Herefordshire. Until I moved to Oxfordshire in 2014, the rest of my life was spent in that 'Marches' region. It's also where my family comes from. My father Alan Bailey's ancestors were blacksmiths and farriers, and my mother Judith was from a farming family.

"That's where my love of nature originates. I spent time as a child running free on my grandparent's farm near Rugeley. My Mum knew a lot about nature, as did my grandparents and I just absorbed it. I remember that, when I was four, I used my pocket money to buy a Ladybird book of garden birds. I don't think I'd take that one to Oxtopia but I do treasure my old RSPB *Birdwatching* book published by Mitchell Beazley. I spent hours and hours outside and became passionate about bird watching. I enjoyed mucking about by the River Wye which is quite beautiful in Herefordshire and is where I was taught fly fishing by one of my school teachers, the Reverend Burgoyne. I performed well enough in school but I always preferred to be outside."

Secondary school was The Bishop of Hereford's Bluecoat Church of England School. Given Estelle's love of the outdoors, readers will not be surprised that she was keen on and good at sport.

"I played hockey and netball for school and county. I was madly into athletics and ran for the county. Unusually for the mid-1980s I loved playing football. It was difficult but I travelled to Droitwich to play for Droitwich St Andrews and for the West Midlands from fourteen to sixteen. In 1985 we went on tour in the USA."

The opportunities for women's football are much better across the Atlantic than in the UK although the situation is improving slowly.

"A couple of years ago I went to a school reunion and was surprised by how the others remembered me. I was a prefect, house captain and games captain in my year and they thought of me as kind of 'square' and saw me in the role of leader,"

But perceptions changed when Estelle unexpectedly left school at sixteen. The reason?

"My father taught at the School of Farriery in Hereford and was building a reputation as a world authority on the subject of Equine Orthotics and was away a lot abroad lecturing. He is semi-retired now but is still involved.

"My mother suffered from post-natal depression. She died in 2009 from a brain tumour and we now believe had been growing for a long time although we were unaware of it. As a teenager I found it hard to cope with her depression, so my love of the outdoors was a form of escapism for me.

"For a few years I became estranged from my family and left home aged sixteen. While living in a homeless hostel, I tried unsuccessfully to study for my 'A' levels at the Sixth Form College."

Life was tough so Estelle looked for a job to try to improve her circumstances but didn't really know what she wanted to do.

"My life changed in 1989 thanks to meeting some lovely 'grounded' people from Presteigne in Wales. They took me under their wing and I moved there and did various part time jobs in the day, working in a dairy as a lab technician and in a couple of factories and in a caring job. In the evenings I studied 'A' level English, Sociology and Law (though she dropped Law). When I finished 'A' levels I took a degree in Environmental Science through the Open University."

Into the wildlife trusts

Estelle first discovered the Wildlife Trusts after she moved to Welshpool in 1995.

"I read an article about Ted Smith, the man who was the driving force behind the development of Wildlife Trusts in the late 1940s and 50s. Ted was an inspiration to me," said Estelle.

"He could see that intensive agriculture, industrial forestry and development were threatening his native Lincolnshire, which was teeming with birds and butterflies. In 1948 he founded the Lincolnshire Wildlife Trust and the following year, with a membership of just 129 people, he created the nature reserve at Gibraltar Point, a coastal belt of sand dunes and salt marsh near Skegness. This was a precious breeding area for plovers and other waders, and under threat from development as a caravan park."

Ted worked tirelessly during the 1950s to help other Wildlife Trusts take shape, including Montgomeryshire Wildlife Trust. "He wanted Wildlife Trusts to encourage people to explore nature reserves and become involved. I was very lucky to meet him last year, and a few months ago he died at the age of 95 – leaving us a wonderful legacy."

In 1998, Estelle started volunteering for the Shropshire and the Montgomeryshire Wildlife Trusts.

"It was a real 'come-home' moment when I discovered what I wanted to do with my life and I have never looked back since."

Estelle was given a six month's contract at the Montgomeryshire Wildlife Trust as Wildlife Sites Officer to conduct a survey of wildlife sites in a given area. This was followed by further short contracts including a habitat survey in the district of Pumlumon. In 2001 she landed a temporary post with The Royal Society of Wildlife Trusts based in Newark. This is the umbrella organisation for all 47 Wildlife Trusts across the UK, with collectively more than 800,000 members and 45,000 volunteers.

Estelle returned to Montgomeryshire to manage the Trust's Heritage Lottery Funded (HLF) Nature Reserves Improvement Project, where she continued to develop a reputation for being an effective manager and good with people. Estelle told me that her secret is being a diligent listener and leading by example.

When the director of Montgomery Wildlife Trust left in 2004, Estelle was appointed Chief Executive in 2005 and was in charge when they received a number of large grants to improve the Pumlumon area. It was a worked-out, barren landscape with few visitors: the natural woodland had vanished and the ancient peat bog, which had soaked up CO_2 for thousands of years, had been drained. Despite the exploitation of the environment, the local economy was weak. What happened in that area affected the floodplains of the River Severn and River Wye and contributed to severe flooding in towns and villages downstream.

Estelle said: "We developed a vision for 40,000 hectares of the uplands and worked on a landscape scale to conserve and repair the broken upland ecosystems. In doing so we aimed to bring back the skylark, long eared owls, stonechats and harriers.

"The Pumlumon Project made me think bigger, to move beyond the size of a small nature reserve to the much wider landscape. The area we took on was the size of Birmingham. We approached insurance companies to help us because they are interested in flood prevention. We were able to develop a 'payment for services fund' to give to local farmers to improve their land."

Estelle is particularly proud of the results of the Dyfi Osprey Project, which is part of the Pumlumon Project.

"In 2005, we erected an osprey nesting platform on Cors Dyfi Nature Reserve, a reserve that I had restored from a former conifer plantation back to a bog under the HLF project. In 2008 we witnessed the first breeding pair of osprey in 500 years in Wales, and since then ospreys have been nesting there every year. Monty, the male bird, was a star on BBC *Springwatch* for three years running. The award-winning 360 Observatory we built in 2013 enables people to get really close to nature and see the osprey nests."

Between 2008 and 2009 Estelle was also sent as a trouble-shooter to Brecknock Wildlife Trust.

"Wildlife Trusts are charities that have to be run like businesses if they are to succeed and survive. For a while I ran both Trusts until a new chief executive was appointed for Brecknock, and I had a similar role in Herefordshire in 2013. "In 2013, I was approached by head-hunters to apply for this post at BBOWT. At the time I was living in Shropshire, an area where I felt rooted, so it was a big decision to move to Oxfordshire."

"Montgomeryshire was one of the smallest Wildlife Trusts and BBOWT is one of the largest with a £5.5 million turnover. But what makes it a pleasure to be the Chief Executive is the people I work with. Wildlife Trust people are passionate and yet down-to-earth lovely people. I enjoy watching people grow, having been on that journey myself from volunteer to now chief executive of one of the largest Trusts."

Estelle marked her second anniversary with BBOWT, and a new five-year Strategic Plan ready to be delivered. So what is her view of the future?

"My aim is to maintain the best of what is happening already but we have to link the environment and social agenda. The roaming area of a typical child is now only 500 yards compared with the five miles when I was a child. We have a big responsibility to reconnect people to nature particularly in urban areas. At BBOWT we get this. Here in Oxford our Wild Oxford project puts on lots of events and empowers people to look at their back gardens to encourage wildlife on their doorsteps. The Oxford Festival of Nature was a massive success in June 2015 with around 6,000 people enjoying more than sixty events. People love nature, and it's our job to help them find it.

"We try to present a spatial picture of how we connect with nature through rivers, through ecosystems and through people. To do that we have community officers to engage people and to get them involved at grassroots inspiring people to undertake local action. The Wild Oxford volunteer teams have built elevated

boardwalks, a pond dipping platform at Rivermead Nature Park, scythed acres of fens, run guided walks, discovered 'lost' plants of the fens and held open days including the Happy Valley Easter picnic at Chilswell Valley."

Pressure building

Estelle and BBOWT face huge strategic challenges across the three counties of Berks, Bucks & Oxon.

"The development pressure is to build on green belt is unceasing and a significant amount of that is planned for Oxfordshire. We have to avoid concreting over the county. If we don't invest in natural resources like water and make sure that ecosystems are connected, we damage those resources irrevocably and can't keep taking them. Companies like Thames Water and BMW depend on a reliable, clean and sustainable water supply. The cost of flooding and pollution isn't just felt by wildlife but by human beings as well.

"We have evolved with nature, and our health and wellbeing is dependent on a healthy natural world. The quality and sustainability of our lives depends on the quality of the air, the water and the soil. We have to provide a 'Natural Health Service' and learn to place the environment at the heart of economic growth."

Our modern world where the value of everything is monetised poses a problem for environmentalists. Estelle has an interesting take on the problem.

Banking on ecosystems

"We should think of the environment as a bank. Like any bank you need to put money in it in order to take out. The state that it is in now is near collapse. Ecosystems are seriously broken. We need to understand the value of nature; that is how people will understand that they have a duty to look after it, and that means paying for it."

"One of our main projects focuses on restoring the Upper Thames because the Thames catchment area faces problems. Wildlife habitat is lost when fields are ploughed up and severe flooding and pollution can occur when chemicals from agriculture run off into the rivers. It costs water companies to clean it up. Having the right wildlife habitats in the right places is good for nature and also good for business and people."

Books would be in Estelle's bag to Oxtopia.

"*The Art of Seeing 2* by Reuters would be there because I think in pictures and people interest me, it's so important to walk with your eyes open. I'm sure Oxtopia is wonderful but I wouldn't want to forget what lies beyond. I would also take *Natural Capital: Why It Matters* by Oxford-based Dieter Helm who is Vice President of the Wildlife Trust and Chair of the Natural Capital Committee, and *What Nature Does for Britain* by Tony Juniper.

Estelle concluded: "I hope Oxtopia is a pristine natural environment despite its ever increasing human population." Having met Estelle, I'm sure she'll inspire Oxtopians to keep it wildlife friendly.

Estelle Bailey

Born: 1970

Occupation: Chief Executive of BBOWT

Castaway Items: Mitchell Beazley *RSPB Birdwatching*; *Natural Capital: Why It Matters* by Oxford-based Dieter Helm; *What Nature Does for Britain* by Tony Juniper

Original OLE Interview: December 2015

For more information on Berkshire, Buckinghamshire and Oxfordshire Wildlife Trust go to www.bbowt.org.uk

Castaway 3:7
Dennis Harrison

"The book is not dead: Long live the book" especially in the hands of Dennis Harrison who runs that precarious passion – a small independent bookshop. Located in Jericho it offers live jazz, world music, slam poetry, silent movies, book clubs, bookbinding classes and 70 varieties of tea...

When a book is just a click away, those independent traditional bookstores that survive have done so by finding innovative ways of communicating their love and knowledge of books. While Oxford's Blackwells store on Broad Street has the aura of a world heritage site, there is another Oxford bookshop tiny in comparison which has become an important part of Oxford's cultural life. And the owner Dennis Harrison has had quite a journey to Oxford himself.

"Mine is the story of a boy who grew up on a rough sort of council estate and ended up going to Christ Church. I always say the estate was the sort of place where you hit someone before you asked 'What are you looking at?'"

Back to the beginning: "I was born in London, in Kilburn," said "and I was two when the family moved out of London. "I grew up in Aylesbury in the 1960s when it was a lovely market town. But I remember Kilburn because we returned often to visit extended family members. My parents were given a grant to get out of London at a time when families like mine of ten or more people were living in two or three rooms.

Dennis passed the 11-plus and went to Aylesbury Grammar School and described his childhood thus: "I see myself as living in the last golden age when children were allowed lots of freedom and I could ride off on my bike and make dens in the woods. I was one of the last beneficiaries of a system of Grammar Schools which enabled social mobility. Today Aylesbury Grammar is more like a private school on the cheap and doesn't have the same effect on social mobility.

"When I was a pupil, the school was unusual because it allowed me to spend time locked away in the music room. I got away with bunking off lessons, my teenage years were about music, music and more music. I had some well respected piano teachers who encouraged me."

Despite his love of classical music and his talent at the piano he chose not to read music at university.

"I wanted to keep music as a hobby because I felt I could never be as good as I wanted to be. History for me was quite dispassionate, quite remote so that it didn't disturb my private interests. That's why I chose to read history."

From council house to Christ Church

Dennis moved from a council house in Aylesbury to the staircases of Christ Church. A culture shock I rather predictably asked?

"I pretended to be urbane: at grammar school I had become used to mixing with people from different backgrounds. But it still took a while to settle in because I was quite shy and Christ Church has a forbidding atmosphere. There aren't many shared facilities. Students are tucked away behind the closed doors of private rooms.

Having gained his history degree, Dennis like so many graduates didn't know what he wanted to do. "But I had a list of things that I didn't want to do. While I made up my mind I worked in Weatherheads Bookshop in Aylesbury. Aesthetically I liked being surrounded by old books. The environment was vibrant and interesting, and it suited me temperamentally."

Music played a part too. "I love jazz, it's immediate, visceral and dangerously unpredictable – all the things that make life wonderful and tragic."

"I organised jazz nights every week at the railway station cafe. They were immense fun. I was able to use churches when I needed bigger venues to accommodate larger audiences. That way I was able to pay the musicians and attract well-known artists." (including Gilad Atzmon, the Israeli born saxophonist and author and now a regular at the Albion, pictured below).

Having accidentally discovered the career he wanted, he decided to set up his own independent bookshop.

"In the 1990s I opened the Wendover Bookshop (in Aylesbury) and started a family. I have three sons, now in their twenties who work in London or are undertaking postgraduate study."

Sylvia with Korky Paul and Victor Glynn at the Albion Beatnik Bookshop, sketch by Weimin He

The advent of online book buying made the Wendover Bookshop harder to sustain. So when the lease ended Dennis looked around for a location with better prospects.

At the Albion Beatnik Bookstore cafe

"Having been a student in Oxford, I knew the city well and loved it. I opened the Albion Beatnik (next to Oxford University Press in Walton Street) in 2008 with the aim of specialising in twentieth-century books."

I wondered how he decided on the name?

"Originally I was to call the shop the Anglican Beatnik, but I supposed people would think I'd be selling fluorescent Bibles, so I settled on the word Albion, which is the oldest name for England. Beatnik is American slang, a mid-twentieth century construct introduced by Beat writer Jack Kerouac in 1948; he claimed its derivation from the word beatific. When I opened I had decided to stock only English and American writing from the twentieth century."

"When I was fitting the shop, I ran out of money and was left with nothing in the middle so I needed to improvise. I bought cheap tables and made shelves out of empty crates which I painted."

Given the great economic crash of the time, it wasn't an auspicious moment to open a bookshop. Dennis says,

"The first eighteen months were desperate but the shop survived. Even in the darkest hours, I could never contemplate closing the shop. When I started the cafe its fortune began to turn."

"I didn't envisage what is has become today. I opened it as a traditional bookshop but the shop took on new life as more people became involved, with many party events often lasting through the night. It became a hippy kingdom without the hippies."

"When Gilad Atzmon was the performer for my second jazz evening in 2011, 85 people turned up and in spite of the heat everyone loved it. Following that success I invited a seven-piece folk band. So many people turned up that the band played outside, emptying the local bars and blocking the road. The police came twice to move the crowd on."

And so the Albion Beatnik evolved into the Mecca it is for poets jazz lovers and bibliophiles today. Surrounded by so many wonderful books I wondered what Dennis would choose to take to Oxtopia.

"I can think of no better way to live or die than listening to Glenn Gould play the Goldberg Variations – probably the 1955 recording which skips."

I explained that there may be a problem with that if the castaways have not succeeded in generating electricity. When I told Dennis that there were two pianos on Oxtopia, he was concerned that he would get little time on them: we agreed that he could take his own Steinway and inside will be hidden the complete works of Shakespeare and of WB Yeats. Dennis played some of the Bach variations for me from memory and said, "I'll write down the music when I arrive on the island so I won't forget it."

Dennis Harrison

Occupation: Bookstore owner

Castaway Items: Glenn Gould playing the Goldberg Variations; a Steinway piano and the complete works of Shakespeare and of WB Yeats

Original OLE Interview: December 2015

The Albion Beatnik Bookstore is at
34 Walton St, Oxford, OX2 6AA
www.albionbeatnik.co.uk

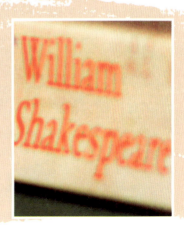

Gillian Cox

When Gillian's father was diagnosed with Alzheimer's disease in 1979, there was little support for sufferers and their families in Oxfordshire then. She is a modest person and would not say it herself but I'm convinced that Vale House – the world's first hospice for sufferers with terminal Alzheimer's disease and their families – would not have happened without her.

Gillian was born in Odd Down, a suburb of Bath, at the beginning of World War 2 in the flat above her father Tom Palmer's chemist shop.

"When nearby Bristol was bombed, my father felt his family would be safer if he moved because the shop was near the railway station. My mother Frances was a teacher but in those days as soon as a woman married she had, by law, to leave teaching. She had met my father and their two best friends at school. Those friends were the parents of my future husband Keith Cox. Keith was six years older than me but because of our parents friendship we met often during childhood. On one occasion he was heard to say of me 'I wouldn't marry her if she was the last person on earth.'"

After taking 'A' levels in Physics, Chemistry, Botany and Zoology, Gillian headed to Bedford College (London University) where she read Biology. She continued, "while I was a student, Keith would drive down from Leeds to take me out in his soft topped red sports car – well his Morris 8!" said Gillian. "It was cool. In fact it was absolutely freezing!"

A happily married teacher

After Gillian graduated Keith did change his mind and they married in 1961. Some years earlier Keith had taken a degree in Geology at The Queens College, Oxford. The practice of geology in the late 1950s didn't involve health and safety regulation and Keith lost an eye while on a field trip in the Lake District but he didn't let it affect his life. He continued his research at Leeds University in the Institute of African Geology, while Gillian taught biology and general science at Leeds Girls High School.

Keith's research involved several trips to southern Africa. "During those trips," said Gillian, "our only way of staying in touch was by air mail. Given the earlier accident, I had to try not to worry."

An idyllic time followed his appointment as lecturer in petrology at Edinburgh University in 1963.

"All three of our children, James Emma and William were born in Scotland where they enjoyed a lot of freedom to roam."

There was a dearth of childcare facilities in the 1960s and 70s, and women began to work together to form the Pre-school Playgroups Association and in Edinburgh Gillian was one of those women.

"I approached a local church to see if we could use their hall but they threw up their hands in horror at the idea of paint, sand and water. I met Mary Ward, a colonel's wife at the local barracks and she too wanted to set up a playgroup. We convened a local PPA branch and established the first one in the area on the Milton Bridge. Barracks"

Then in 1972, Keith became a lecturer in geology at Oxford and was made a fellow of Jesus College the following year.

"We bought our house in Kennington where I have lived ever since. Keith was appointed a Reader in 1988 which was an exciting time because in the same year he became a Fellow of the Royal Society."

Gillian explained that their time in Edinburgh had given them a deep love of Scotland and that was where they liked to holiday. Keith lived a life of adventure but, in August 1998, he tragically lost his life in a sailing accident off the Isle of

Mull. In his obituary in The Independent, Keith was described as "one of the most influential geologists of his generation because of the range of interests and expertise which he combined with a powerful intellect." But the obituary also gives a sense of the person that Gillian had fallen in love with.

"Cox was a warm, friendly man, respected by all and held in some awe, not only by students... His humour was delightfully spiced with light irony and he liked nothing better than to prick pompous balloons. He was widely read, a gifted musician, playing the piano, clarinet and guitar, and as something of a bon viveur enjoyed good food and wine and defiantly puffed his pipe at tea-time."

It must have helped Gillian a great deal to have had such a genial companion because in 1979 she faced an unexpected and difficult situation. Her teaching career in the area had already faced several challenges. A difficult term at Redfield School in Blackbird Leys had been followed by a period as acting Head of Science and Maths at Donnington Middle School. She then moved to Abingdon College of Further Education where she taught Human Biology for twenty years mostly on the Access Course which enabled mature students to study at Oxford Brookes University. When her mother died from rheumatoid arthritis in 1974 her father moved to the Oxford area and, the responsibility for his care as well as the care of her children and the demands of a career in teaching fell on Gillian.

Alzheimer's: The search for a caring culture

Soon after he retired in 1979 Tom Palmer, was diagnosed as having Alzheimer's. Gillian said, "The word 'Alzheimer's was hardly used at that time but the reality of it was understood – and my father's behaviour was becoming difficult to manage. So, when Dr Gordon Wilcox held a meeting for carers and relatives, I was keen to attend."

From that meeting in 1980, the Oxfordshire branch of the Alzheimer's Disease Society was formed with Gillian as chair. She was followed as chairwoman by Joan King who was to work closely with Gillian in founding Vale House.

"For many of us, that led to a desire to do something practical. In 1984 we opened a day centre, the Abingdon Alzheimer's Club."

By the time Gillian's father died in 1984 she understood the need for special care in the advanced stages of the disease. Gillian had toured homes which would take in patients with terminal Alzheimer's but she came away distressed. She had seen instances of patients tied to chairs or dosed with chemical restraints. Gillian said,

"Encouraged and supported by Steve Corea, the Assistant Director of Mental Health Services, Joan King and I went to see how people elsewhere in the country were tackling the problem. There were some homes with specialist wings but nowhere devoted to the sole care of patients with dementia. We felt there was an unmet need and set ourselves the target of raising £120,000.

"The three local patrons who supported our appeal were the Duke of Marlborough, Sir Patrick Nairn and John Patten MP. In 1990, we were awarded first prize of

£20,000 by a telethon appeal on Central TV. Help from the Vale of White Horse District Council meant we eventually reached £200,000. They also made part of Field House on the Botley Road available to us. That is why we named it Vale House as a way of saying 'thank you'."

Iris Murdoch and other stories

So Gillian and her team succeeded in establishing Vale House: the first home of its kind in the country. It was fully occupied and officially opened, on 20 November 1990, by Diana Princess of Wales. One of the former residents was that wonderful Oxford storyteller Iris Murdoch. If you saw the 2001 film Iris about her descent into memory loss, you may remember the character of Tricia. Tricia (O'Leary) is the Head of Vale House and Gillian was chair of the governors when they made that inspired appointment, in 1993. I had the privilege of casting away Sister Frances Domenica, the founder of the first hospice for children and I sensed that Tricia shared a similar devotion to the Vale House project. Indeed Gillian said "Vale House with Tricia at its head is regarded as an international model for the care of people with dementia. It is the only care home in Oxfordshire to be judged 'Outstanding' by the Care Quality Commission"

Gillian and her team wanted to establish a philosophy of care.

"As well as involving the family in the patient's care, we wanted each resident to have a personal book. In effect that book was to contain a record of his/her life with photographs, memorabilia and stories."

"While attending a conference at Nottingham University I heard about Reminiscence Therapy. We felt that knowing who the patient was and stories about him/her could help deliver respectful individualised care and that it should be part of the ethos of Vale House."

For practical reasons, and with respect for their residents, a recorded life history can have special meaning for those trying to help persons needing special care at the end of their lives.

So what would Gillian take with her to the mythical island of Oxtopia? Her love of music has helped raise her spirits during hard times. She sings with Oxford Harmonic and told me "I'll need a piano and lots of music on the island."

She also wanted to take a carved oriental chest in her hallway. "My parents married in Penang (Malaysia) in 1935. Having lost two babies, my mother was advised to return to England. Soon after they left, Malaya was invaded by the Japanese and many of their friends died in camps in Burma."

That chest travelled with Gillian's parents from Asia. It looked to me like a symbol of survival. In the end we agreed that she could take the chest filled with books that she wouldn't want to be without lots of sheet music. Gillian also wanted the brass pestle and mortar from her father's shop which he loved, and on Oxtopia it would be a reminder of him, but he most precious object inside the chest would be one of Keith's paintings.

"Keith enjoyed painting and planned to do more when he retired. I would want to take one of his paintings to Oxtopia. We also enjoyed bird watching. Maybe I could have a pair of binoculars around my neck when you send me to the island?"

Gillian Cox

Born: 1939

Occupation: Teacher and charity organiser and founder

Castaway Items: carved oriental chest; piano; brass pestle and mortar; husband's painting

Original OLE Interview: August 2016

Don Manley

A crossword compiler would make an excellent addition to the castaway community: and Duck, Pasquale, Quixote, Bradman, Giovanni, and Izetti (his many aliases depending for whom he is setting his puzzles) is such a man.

Donald Manley's agile mind likes to challenge us, for Donald, who prefers to be called Don, is a crossword setter. In a foreword to Don's book the Chambers Crossword Manual, another renown Oxford-based crossword compiler his friend and rival Colin Dexter described a train journey they took together to record a television programme, called Crosstalk.

"At Oxford station, Don bought *The Times*, the *Independent*, *The Guardian*, *The Daily Telegraph*: without any assistance from me he had completed them all before we reached Reading. Twenty three minutes."

But Don thinks the journey might have taken a bit longer than that. Don's story doesn't begin in Oxford but in Cullompton in Devon where he was born.

Rural Roots

"My father, Chave was a commercial traveller selling animal medicines to West Country farms and my mother Alma was a farmer's daughter, so my roots are rural," Don recalled. "We rarely took a holiday so between terms I often accompanied my dad on his rounds visiting farms and came to appreciate the Devon and Somerset countryside. My father took the *Telegraph*, the *Daily Express* and the *Daily Mail* and did all the crosswords. On Sunday afternoons we'd solve The *Radio Times* puzzle together. I was beginning to get the hang of cryptic puzzles by the age of about thirteen."

"I attended the town's primary school and, after passing the eleven plus exam, I went to Tiveton Grammar School. My older sister Jean became a teacher and she suggested I take the entrance exam for a foundation scholarship to Blundell's"[an independent school named one of the wealthiest merchants from the wool trade of Elizabethan England who died in 1601].

Attending in 1958 with a scholarship for boys of limited means, Don continued: "I felt rather an outsider in the public school culture and sometimes catch that feeling in Oxford, too. In my time a lot of the boys went into the army and everyone was 'volunteered' into the school's Cadet Corps in which with my knowledge of physics rather than warfare, I rose to the rank of sergeant."

"More my thing was the school play. I remember playing Dogberry in *Much Ado about Nothing.* In the cast, as one of my henchmen, was Robert Fox who became a distinguished journalist and covered the Falklands War for the BBC.

Don's first crossword

Don went on to study physics at Bristol University in 1963 but not before he had his first crossword published aged seventeen in *The London Evening News.*

"A visitor drew my attention to the fact that anyone could submit a crossword for publication. I remember the excitement of receiving a Coutts Bank cheque in the post for two guineas."

"I noticed that the cryptic puzzles in the *Radio Times* had a different setter each week so I assumed they were sent in by readers. I thought there was no reason why I shouldn't send them one. I sent several but when they were all rejected, I wrote asking the reason. They explained that they were too untidy and on scrappy paper. So I improved my presentation and it worked – they published the first one I'd sent in 1964. My first clue in the 15-by-15 grid for the *Radio Times* was: 'Doctor refuses to work for TV series (10) [solution at end of interview!]. After that they accepted several more. However Don added "On the morning Neil Armstrong landed on moon, I received a letter from The Radio Times telling me that they wouldn't be publishing any more crossword puzzles so that was it for a while."

The life scientific

The physics department at Bristol where Don studied was led by a Nobel Prize winner, Professor C.F. Powell. After graduating in 1966, Don went to work as a research engineer for the Standard Telecommunications Laboratories in Harlow.

"It was the birthplace of optical fibre communications. A lot of brilliant scientists – of whom I was not one – worked for the company. It was a good experience for me learning to live on my own and meet people of different backgrounds, beliefs and circumstances. I grew up fast in those four years but felt that I should look for a new career. I didn't want to go into teaching – even though my mother had bought me an academic gown when I graduated – just in case I decided to teach!"

"My first idea was to study computer programming but then I thought 'Why not do something using my language skills?' I was offered a publishing job in Stevenage with the Institute of Electrical Engineering but didn't fancy living in another new town. Then I saw a post advertised also in publishing at The Institute of Physics in Bristol. I applied and was accepted. Since then I've been a verbal engineer."

"I joined a church community there and made new friends. One in particular, Susan Richardson, from Northern Ireland, had a PhD in biochemistry and so we were introduced. That was 1972 and we married in at Christ Church Clifton a year later."

Don and Susan's children Richard and Gilly were born in Bristol. Richard is a tax accountant in Salisbury and Gilly lives in London and is a television producer. Gilly

directed a lot of episodes of *The Apprentice*. She has two children Ferris and Gilby and Jonathan has a daughter, Charlotte.

Don spent seven years editing The Journal of Physics D: Applied Physics an important peer reviewed publication. In between being a dad, when the publishing became less challenging, he was tempted to renew his interest in crossword setting.

Back to the crosswords

"I resumed with very hard crossword puzzles for *Games and Puzzles* and *The Listener*. I made fifty of them which were published under my new identity of 'Duck'." Don believes the use of aliases probably spread from the literary tradition via Edward Powys Mathers who was a poet and in 1926 assumed the name Torquemada for his puzzles in The Observer.

Wanting a change from journal editing and a new challenge, Don and his family moved to Cheltenham in 1989. He joined a young educational publishers called Stanley Thornes where he commissioned and edited their first successful science textbook for schools. From there he moved to Oxford to Blackwell and then to Oxford University Press (OUP). Don said

"Thornes took over Blackwell's educational publishing and OUP took over Nelson Thornes so all the books I ever published are now with OUP where I finished up!"

"I was fortunate too in that I inherited a house from a maiden aunt. Once the sitting tenants left, just before we moved to Oxford I was able to sell it and our Cheltenham house and use the proceeds to put a deposit on a house in Hayward Road. Without that, we couldn't have afforded a home in OX2."

Oxford seems to be the beating heart of the crossword world because Jonathan Crowther (well known crossword compiler) and Colin Dexter also live in Oxford. Don described the crossword culture as friendly but there are divisions of opinion when it comes to what is a fair clue. In any event a few later Don was introduced to Betty Kirkpatrick from Chambers "and a few years later, she commissioned me to write *Chambers Crossword Manual*," Don continued, "it was a gamble for them when first published in 1986 but it stayed in print until 2010. Now, to my surprise, I am working on a new edition for Hodder who took over Chambers.

2002 was an 'annus horribilis' for the Manleys. Susan had grown a successful research career as a bio-chemist specialising in Type 2 Diabetes. When her immediate boss died the research grant ended. At the same time, Gilly was made redundant by the Ministry of Sound and Don was made redundant from OUP. He said,

Colin Dexter collaborations

"At the time I was publishing textbooks and revision guides for minority 'A' level subjects like psychology and religious education and OUP decided to stop publishing new ones. On the day I was told of my redundancy, they offered me a taxi home which I declined preferring to cycle up the Banbury Road calling on my friend Colin Dexter on the way.

"Colin also persuaded me to be 'Quixote' in *The Oxford Times* in the 1980s. At that time Colin also set for The Oxford Times under the pseudonym 'Codex'.

Colin makes his Inspector Morse a keen crossword solver and also used crosswords as part of the plot for *The Silent World of Nicolas Quinn*. "We discussed the background detail for that book and I contributed ideas to a couple of others. Colin attributed a clue to me as *The Oxford Times* 'Quixote' even though he wrote the clue himself: it was' Bradman's famous duck'." [The solution is, of course 'Donald'].

Prolific puzzle setter

"Although, in 2002, I still had a mortgage to pay, I decided to take the risk of making crossword compiling my main occupation and rang up *The Daily Telegraph*. They agreed to take me on as a floater but, after two years, I replaced the retiring Ruth Crisp, the Friday setter. I also helped set up the new Telegraph tough-line puzzle where I am called 'Giovanni'. In The Guardian, I am 'Pasquale' and in The Times' Jumbo puzzle I am anonymous but in T2 I am 'Izetti' (from Donizetti). In *The Financial Times* I'm Bradman. I have set well over 1,000 consecutive puzzles for *The Independent* and *The Independent on Sunday*. For over twenty-five years I have been the crossword editor of the *Church Times*. On a typical day I manage one puzzle per day at best two. Over the last eleven years I have over 70,000 clues stored on my computer database."

Ramble on

Since compiling crosswords is a solitary mostly indoor occupation, Don sought midweek exercise walking with the Ramblers. He soon became a walk leader. And until recently he was walks organiser of the Oxford Ramblers. I first met Don out walking with them and noticed that when he leads a walk he has two likeable if somewhat eccentric habits.

Don explained why he taps a tree or post on either side with his stick half way round a walk. "It is in honour of my father. He wasn't a great walker but he would take me on the same rather boring walk every Sunday up the A38 and when we turned back that is what he did."

Don's other request as a walk leader is that when he blows a whistle walkers stop talking – as walkers do and instead listen to the sounds and silence of nature.

"I have had to resign from my organising role because of the work involved in the new edition of *The Chambers Crossword Manual*. It will have a particular emphasis on the history of crosswords coming as it does 100 years after the first one."

Thinking Oxtopia might be an ideal refuge for a crossword compiler I asked Don what he might take with him: "A cricket ball to practice my mostly unsuccessful leg breaks. I'm mad about cricket. I used to be an enthusiastic cricketer although useless at it. I heard England win the Ashes while sitting in my father's car on the Somerset levels in August 1953 – a definitive moment in my youth along with the Coronation, the ascent of Everest and Roger Bannister breaking the four-minute mile.

At that moment the grandfather clock in the room struck and Don smiled. "My father knew fifty poems by heart and every Sunday morning he recited them one after the other so that he didn't forget them. They included some Kipling and the whole of *Gray's Elegy* Written in a Country Churchyard. That's why I want to take that clock. He started reciting as soon as he had shaved and expected to finish when the clock struck the hour. If I heard it strike on the island it would transport me back to my childhood."

And one final clue to take to Oxtopia and baffle the castaways? No fellow for mixing (4,4). Solution see below....

Don Manley

Born: 1945

Occupation: Crossword compiler

Castaway Items: cricket ball, grandfather clock

Original OLE Interview: July 2014

Crossword answers: 'Moonstrike'; and 'lone wolf' (i.e. anagram of no fellow)

THE COMMON THREAD
JOHN SULSTON & GEORGINA FERRY

A computer called LEO

MAX PERUTZ
AND THE SECRET OF LIFE   PIMLICO

GINA FERRY

HY HODGKIN   a life   GEORGINA FERRY

Georgina Ferry

Journalist, author and broadcaster Georgina Ferry champions science and scientists past and present. She was cast away to Oxtopia appropriately in the month of Oxford International Women's Festival and Georgina is passionate about encouraging women to follow careers in science.

Georgina Ferry knows a thing or two about science and women having also written a biography of Dorothy Crowfoot Hodgkin, the only British woman to win a Nobel Prize in science (1964). Georgina's *Dorothy Hodgkin: A Life* captures Dorothy's engaging personality, her immense dedication to research and her connection with the issues of the day. Georgina researches her subjects with similar hard work and dedication and has managed to cope with a demanding career and bringing up a family.

She was born in Hong Kong in 1955, when her father Peter Ferry was a junior officer in The Royal Artillery.

"Army life is peripatetic. I went to four different schools before I was eleven. I was at a primary school in Malaysia with British, Ghurkha, Australian and New Zealand children, so early on I acquired a sense of how big the world is."

"As an upbringing there were advantages and disadvantages: you give up forming intense friendships because you know you are going to leave. You become adaptable, but also somewhat self-contained, " she added.

Georgina went on to board at Ellerslie School for Girls in Great Malvern. "I drifted between the arts and sciences, though I think my instincts were always more on the literary side. I took Physics with Chemistry at 'O' level thinking I might like to become a vet, but changed my mind and took English, French and History at 'A' level. My school encouraged me to apply for Oxford but it had little experience of Oxbridge entrance and neither of my parents had been to university. My father actually thought it was a waste of money for girls to take degrees. So as a seventeen-year-old I tried to negotiate the system with no advice. I applied to read Experimental Psychology, thinking (wrongly) it would give me insight into human nature. Usually non-scientists studied psychology jointly with philosophy, but I felt strongly that the alternative option of physiology would provide a better basis for understanding the brain. At the interview at Lady Margaret Hall (LMH), Alison Brading who became my tutor asked me 'What is the function of water in the body?' My one-word answer – 'Transport' – drove me onto the course."

After graduating in 1976, Georgina went to Washington DC where her father was working as a defence attaché at the British Embassy.

"I was having a lovely time working in a bookshop on Capitol Hill when my tutor contacted me. She had recommended me for the post of research assistant in a laboratory in London. I took the job purely on her recommendation, without application or interview. My boss assumed that I would do a PhD but the project didn't seem to me to be important and anyway a life in research did not appeal. So I looked for other jobs that would make use of my science."

Spreading the word of science

Publishers Chapman & Hall, who had been Dickens's publishers, then specialised in science and technology and they were advertising for a copy editor. Georgina applied and got the job.

"I enjoyed it immensely. I loved the moment when a finished book was placed in my hands for the first time. I've never lost that delight in the smell and feel of a new book. I probably would have stayed in publishing if my partner and future husband David Long hadn't pointed to an advertisement in 1979 for the post of book review editor at the *New Scientist*, saying 'you could do that'."

David and Georgina had met at a Jesus-LMH drama society sherry party during their first week in Oxford – in 1973 all the colleges were single sex. They had spent most of their spare time as students in theatrical productions, she as an actor, he as a lighting designer.

With nothing to lose, Georgina took up David's challenge, applied and was called for an interview.

"To my surprise I got the job. I was only twenty-three, with no experience in journalism, and suddenly I had seven pages a week to fill with reviews and contributors' columns. For the first few months I used to cycle to work weeping with anxiety, but I learned on the job, and eventually began to write news and feature articles on neuroscience."

Soon afterwards Georgina heard of an opening for an occasional presenter on the *Radio 4* programme *Science Now*. She joined the team, anchoring the programme every five weeks while holding down her *New Scientist* job.

At this point Georgina asked if she could take a radio to Oxtopia. I thought maybe a wind-up radio could work.

Science Now and *Oxford Today*

"From all the bewildering variety of media, radio is the one I always return to. It creates images in your head and allows the space for you to think about what you are hearing. The experience of writing scripts was an excellent training in writing short, clear, simple sentences."

"It also gave me valuable experience interviewing scientists across the whole range of disciplines. It was a topical programme and the subject could be anything for particle physics to immunology. The trick is to get the interviewee to explain the science until you understand it yourself – then there's a good chance the audience will too. One memorable interview was with John Kendrew and

Max Perutz who shared the Nobel Prize for work on the structure of proteins. I sensed their professional rivalry. Max Perutz was a devoted friend of Dorothy Hodgkin and I later wrote his biography too."

In 1981 David and Georgina married, and moved from London to Oxford. The following year, Georgina went freelance following the birth of her son Edward. She continued to write features for *New Scientist*. "One of the topics I took on was gender and science – 1984 was the first 'Women into Science and Engineering Year,'" she added.

At the same time she was writing and presenting radio documentaries for the BBC, and found herself doing a lot of travelling once more. Her second son Will was born in 1985, and Georgina began to feel that she needed work closer to home. Oxford University had just launched *Oxford Today* with Christine Hardiment as editor.

"I rang her up and offered an article on Susan Greenfield – this was before Susan became famous [as a neuroscientist]. From then on I wrote a science feature for each issue, and began to build connections across Oxford's science departments. In 1990 the University made me its first Press Officer, so I had the fun of setting up an office where, if journalists rang up, they were actually made welcome. Dealing with the demands of the American press for details of Bill Clinton's student days during the 1993 Presidential election was particularly memorable."

Enter Dorothy Hodgkin

In 1994, Georgina returned to freelance writing having decided to mark the thirtieth anniversary of Dorothy Hodgkin's Nobel Prize with a feature about her in Oxford Today. Although Dorothy was too frail to interview, Georgina sent the family a copy of the magazine article. Georgina continued, "Dorothy died

Dorothy Hodgkin with her family

a month later but her daughter, Liz, wrote to me saying they had been able to read her the article. And she had appreciated it. I visited Liz at the family home in Crab Mill in Warwickshire. Dorothy had an instant claim to fame as the only British woman to win a Nobel Prize in science, but there was no biography of her. I just knew I had to write it."

The Contemporary Scientific Archives Centre had acquired Dorothy's professional papers and they were kept in Bodleian. Jeannine Alton who used to write arts reviews for *The Oxford Times* was a highly skilled cataloguer of scientific papers and she had catalogued Dorothy's papers. "She was also a dear neighbour of mine until her death in 2007," says Georgina, "and I still miss her."

"I wanted to write a rounded biography to answer the question 'How was a woman born in 1910, when opportunities for women in science were almost non-existent, able to reach such heights – and in chemistry, the most male dominated field? I had abundant material because the Hodgkin family rarely threw things away. Dorothy had an unorthodox marriage. She and her husband Thomas were often apart for months at a time and they wrote to each other every day. When Dorothy wanted to write about her work to Thomas – a non-scientist – she explained things simply and described her feelings and difficulties with people and equipment, things you never get from the published scientific record."

Dorothy's chosen field was X-ray crystallography, a technique than reveals the three-dimensional arrangement of atoms inside crystals, and so gives insight into how they work. She was particularly interested in crystals of biological molecules such as penicillin, vitamin B12 and insulin.

"The techniques of the time couldn't get you the whole way there", says Georgina. "She had to begin by imagining possible structures in her head in three dimensions. But it was the aesthetic qualities of crystals that set her off on the path of wanting to be a scientist. She first grew crystals from colourless liquids at the age of ten at a little school in Suffolk, and marvelled at the resulting brilliant colours."

"Scientists are faced with a problem to solve. You have different materials and equipment but what to do with them involves creative thinking and practical innovation. That kind of imagination and creativity is what Dorothy had in spades."

Dorothy Hodgkin: A Life was published by Granta in 1998, and was reissued last year, in time for the 50th anniversary of her Nobel Prize, by Bloomsbury Reader. We discussed what Dorothy might have chosen to take with her to Oxtopia. Georgina said, "I suspect she would most have wanted a trowel and a microscope so that she could work on the island. Her colleague Eleanor Dodson told me 'Dorothy never tired of peering down her microscope and it was one of the possessions she kept when she officially retired.'

BBC Radio 4 marked the 50th anniversary of Dorothy's Nobel Prize with a series, *An Eye for Pattern*, based on Dorothy's correspondence with family and colleagues. With all her biographical and radio experience, Georgina herself helped to select the extracts and introduced the dramatised readings.

Much of Dorothy Hodgkin's working life had been spent in rooms in the Oxford University Museum of Natural History. In 2010 Georgina was invited to be writer in residence to mark their 150th anniversary. Among other projects, she started a blog about objects and activities in the Museum.

'Social' science

"Science is a tremendously social activity. It is possibly the fault of historians who depicted scientists such as Newton and Einstein as lone geniuses that this is often ignored. Modern science is usually collaborative and the interchange is international. The other thing people fail to understand is that science is creative. That misunderstanding is partly due to the fact that science education in schools is involving less and less practical work."

Georgina channels her desire to enthuse people with the joy and creativity of science into her role as Deputy Chair of The Oxford Trust, the charity founded by Sir Martin and Audrey, Lady Wood that works in schools and the community as Science Oxford.

"If I could take one thing from the Museum to Oxtopia, it would be a prehistoric hand axe from the Oxfordshire geology collections. I remember being struck that someone living near Eynsham more than 200,000 years ago, an early ancestor of our own species Homo sapiens, had made it and it is beautiful and useful. It fits in the hand, which gives you a powerful connection to its maker. It was the tool of its day, just as Dorothy's microscopes and X-ray tubes were the tools of hers."

"I'd also love to take my British Moth dinghy that I sail on the Thames by Port Meadow. I love the natural world so a pair of binoculars could be a good idea. As Dorothy has had my attention for many years of my life, her model of penicillin (now in the Museum of the History of Science) would be an fascinating possibility." Georgina doubted that Hodgkin would care much about possessions in Oxtopia, "She was the least materialistic of people. She went to the States for three months in 1947 taking only one suitcase and most of that was filled with her model of penicillin."

Georgina Ferry

Born: 1955

Occupation: Science writer and broadcaster

Castaway Items: 200,000 year old hand axe; a wind-up radio; British Moth dinghy; Dorothy Hodgkin's model of penicillin

Original OLE Interview: March 2015

Castaway 3:11

Jeremy Spafford

There are arts organisations and there are homeless charities and there is the Old Fire Station Arts Centre, a combination of both. This castaway is the director of a unique Oxford facility.

The Old Fire Station (OFS) is four years old. That may not seem a long time but for the OFS that is an achievement of some magnitude. When it opened with this extraordinary vision, many nay-sayers couldn't envisage people with homes and homeless people sharing a space and both feeling comfortable within it. For that reason, the OFS was launched with hope at its heart but looking doomed without public subsidy to guarantee its future. Jeremy Spafford, its current director, said:

"We were ruthless at hiring space and raising funds from social investors to survive for three months at a time, then for six months at a time and now that we are getting stronger we aim to survive year by year."

"We offer a public space which is shared by very different people which helps to break down barriers. We help homeless people choose their own labels by including them as audience, participant, trainee, volunteer, contributor or artist. This develops networks, build resilience and leads to more stable lives."

Training and support

This unusual venue has succeeded on all fronts, as Jeremy explained: "Our reputation depends on providing good quality art aimed at adults, art events which take risks, asks questions and entertains. Our audiences come to have fun and to enjoy quality performances but they don't distinguish between the professional actors and the homeless people who take part in them."

Today, twenty-seven regular dance classes take place there every week, and it hosts mainstream and experimental shows and exhibitions. The Crisis café, which also trains homeless people, serves delicious freshly cooked food at modest prices. The OFS gives much needed support to early- and mid-career artists from all disciplines. It provides advice, subsidy, networks and promotion to help them become more successful. That this is all happening and that the lives of many homeless people have been transformed is, in part, due to the leadership of Jeremy Spafford and his life journey which has prepared him to head this unusual organisation. In a way Jeremy is the perfect fit for the OFS.

Jeremy's journey

"I was born in Hebden Bridge in Yorkshire. It's become a trendy place to live but back in 1959 when I was born this old mill town was dying. My dad, Christopher Spafford was the vicar. He told me how he was shown around the great hope for the town, the newly built asbestos factory which turned out to be a disaster. I didn't stay there for long because my dad became Rector of Thornhill. We then moved to Shrewsbury. My father died a few years ago and his last post was Provost of Newcastle Cathedral."

"My mother Stephanie's maiden name was Peel and she could trace her family back to Sir Robert Peel the founder of the police and of the income tax. Both my parents came from well to do cotton families. My father traced his family even further back to a cobbler who fought on the side of Harold's brother against Harold at the battle of Stamford Bridge before his defeat at the battle of Hastings."

Jeremy showed me an 18th-century metal card case engraved with the name of Father Henry Garnet and made to commemorate him. Father Henry Garnet was an English Jesuit priest convicted in the Gunpowder Plot of 16056. Jeremy's grandmother was a Garnet and through her he has direct connections to those events celebrated with fireworks on November 5. Jeremy said,

"Henry Garnet was executed. When his head hit the straw the blood from it was reputed to have formed the shape of the head of Christ.

"I was brought up in a working class Yorkshire town but I lived in a middle class island in that community: the vicarage. One of the things I treasure about the way my parents brought me up is their strong values. They weren't interested in money or status but they were interested in people and, whatever their background, they related to them.

"I was sent to a convent primary school but, given my father's peripatetic career, they sent me to a boarding prep school when I was eight. It was hard. I did okay there but when I look back on it: it was a violent place where it was routine for the teachers to hit children constantly. But there were some committed teachers and because of that I enjoyed lots of it. Once we moved to Shrewsbury, I became a day boy at Shrewsbury School. I enjoyed the school for most of the time but towards the end I became disillusioned by the privilege and the sense of entitlement we were encouraged to adopt."

"My exam results weren't as good as expected. My father and my elder brothers Martin and Tim had been to Oxford. I didn't do well enough for Oxford and that coincided with my parents moving to Newcastle where my father became Provost. I went from a posh public school to Walls End Technical College to retake my 'A' levels in English, History and German."

Exploring drama

"I suddenly found myself among people who would find public school a complete mystery. It was helpful grounding being surrounded by young people less privileged and cleverer than me. "

Jeremy was offered a place at Exeter University to study English and Drama. His love of acting was shared by his family. "We all enjoyed acting and I performed in every school play since the year dot. In the sixth form, I played Thomas More in *A Man for all Seasons* and Bolingbrook in *Henry IV*."

"The course at Exeter was unusual and it changed my life. A group of ten of us were in a studio for three years exploring drama in an intense way. We studied primitive theatre using masks. We looked at body language and learned how to move and communicate in a space .It was therapeutic in lots of ways –an inside out training which involved learning about myself, finding an internal honesty and being able to communicate with audiences at a deep level.

"On my first day I met Kirsten (Baker). She was named after a Swedish opera star. We met in the drama studio and in our second year we moved in together and we have been partners for 37 years. I became politicised and active in student politics and Kirsten was an active feminist. The second time I met her she was wearing a badge which said 'A woman needs a man like a fish needs a bicycle.' For her fiftieth birthday I commissioned a sculpture from Darren Greenhow and Fish on a Bicycle stands in our garden in Rose Hill. It has to be a possibility for the desert island," said Jeremy.

"After university I found work in Newcastle with a theatre group called Skin and Bones. We did some rather bad community theatre in and around Newcastle. Kirsten found work as an actress in Manchester and went on to lecture in drama at Manchester University. We wanted to be together and I came to the conclusion that I didn't have a strong enough commitment to the peripatetic life of an actor. I wanted roots. When, as a child, I was asked what I wanted to be when I grew up I always answered, 'I want to be a dad.' I never really had a plan.

"I moved to Manchester and went to work as an auxiliary in a mental hospital which was in a former workhouse. I trained as a psychiatric nurse. This was the early 1980s and there was a lot wrong with the system. There were women in the hospital who had been committed because they had illegitimate babies and became trapped there. I became passionate about the rights of people in those situations. In the mid-1980s I was given a good post helping people to get out of those institutions.

"In 1990 Kirsten decided to become a midwife and that was how we came to Oxford because she trained at Oxford Brookes. By then we had three children under five. Friends put us up until we found a place in Florence Park and I found work with Oxford Housing Aid Centre, a charity which helped homeless young people. In the early 1990s it worked out of a office cabin opposite this building (OFS)

"I went on to work for the homeless charity Centrepoint which is the national youth homeless charity. When I left after seven years, I was in a senior management position. In 1998 I went freelance and for the next thirteen years I was a management consultant to businesses mainly in the public and third sectors. I advised most cultural and social organisations in Oxfordshire and was asked to help with service development, facilitation, evaluation and team building. I joined the board of Pegasus Theatre and was also the founding chair of a charity called Connection which works with individuals with different needs including mental health and drug problems or learning disability and it helps them to become independent. It started in Oxford and now operates across Oxfordshire and Buckinghamshire.

"I also did some theatre work because I used theatre in training. I wasn't looking for a job but two days before the deadline I saw an advertisement for the post of director of a new project – the OFS – which aimed to combine an arts centre with working with the homeless. This was a job that was unlikely to come around twice and it combined everything I was interested in."

A cause for celebration

Jeremy applied and unsurprisingly was appointed director of this new creation which opened in November 2011. It draws on all the threads from Jeremy's past roles as actor, psychiatric nurse, advisor to the homeless and management consultant.

"What I love about the OFS is that it is a place where through art and culture people can celebrate the good bits of life. I have spent so much of my life working with misery and with people with needs and issues. What is great about this place is that we don't talk about homelessness but about colours, fun, creativity and what the individual is good at.

"On one hand the OFS is a traditional arts centre open to the public, with an eclectic mixture of activities and workshops. It is accessible and affordable whether you want performance poetry, theatre, dance, visual arts, to shop for contemporary craft or have lunch in the café but we do it all in a building we share with Crisis. We don't keep that a secret we celebrate it. The homeless people who come in here have as much contribution to make as anyone else. The combination has been a complete non-issue. Most homeless people would feel uncomfortable wandering into an arts centre and most arts centre goers would feel scared walking into a night shelter. But here, whether you come in for a nice coffee, to buy an attractive necklace, to take part in a dance class or are homeless and have come for a literacy class or training, you have come to the right place. You are not treading on someone else's territory."

I asked Jeremy to tell me more about the work with homeless people.

"Because of the range of activities available our training scheme offers opportunities in customer service and retail as well as in art and theatre. If they do well in the café or the shop we are able to give them a good reference to help them into employment. We encourage homeless people to be volunteer ushers. Like the Playhouse, we have students and retired people as theatre ushers but we also encourage homeless people to be volunteer ushers and they enjoy being part of the team. They realise we rely on them and learn the importance of good timekeeping. We do all this through our partnership with Crisis."

Art classes have a different focus from many in the world of social services. Jeremy explained: "In social work the focus is on the process and on fun. But the product isn't that important. We don't do that. We tell them that you can come out of that 'homeless class' and can work with a professional and become as obsessed with product as with process. An example of that is the cut steel sculpture on the wall in the foyer."

Homeless people worked with artists Rachel Barbaresi and Emma Reynard to create this impressive work of art. They visited the Botanic Garden and made sketches and outlines of leaves and flowers. The steel cut outs were based on them. Jeremy said,

"The participants enjoyed it so much .One of them was a recovering heroin addict. She went on to do the foundation art course in the College of Further Education and from there to study art at Camberwell. The experience turned her life around. An older guy who was involved in the same project had never been in the Botanic Garden. He hadn't seen it as a place that would welcome him. He was inspired to buy a season pass and to me someone having access to a place that enhances their life is just as important as going on to study."

At the time I interviewed Jeremy, the OFS was abuzz with preparations for *Before the Tempest* – a prequel to *The Tempest* and directed by Lizzy McBain. Jeremy said,

"It is part of our 'Hidden Spire' project now in its third year. At the heart of this building is the hose tower where the hoses were hung to dry out. It has become the stair well. It is a tower in the middle of Oxford. It exists but it is a hidden dreaming spire. Each year the Hidden Spire project results in a performance on stage and we have been working on it for over a year. It involves professional writers, designers, a director and three professional actors. Fifty-six different homeless people are involved in the production: some from the beginning in the writing process and others work backstage later in the year. It is on for four nights in mid-September. There are seven people on stage: three professional actors and the other four are homeless people. We charge to see the show but we are charging for a product that is of a high standard and is worth paying to see."

We had talked about Jeremy's work at the OFS but not about his lifelong ambition to be a dad.

"At the age of fourteen our eldest son Jos declared that he wanted to be a professional contemporary dancer. I didn't think that would be possible but he proved me wrong. He is a successful contemporary dancer based in Brussels and has toured South Korea. Last year his company won an Olivier award. Louis is a landscape gardener and happy settled with his partner. Martha until recently worked at The Pegasus Theatre. She has just returned from volunteering in Palestine. She's one of those young people who want to make the world a better place. Our youngest daughter, Dora is in her second year at Bristol University learning Portuguese and French. She has passed her driving test and I've realised that I no longer have any teenage children: they are all adults now."

So what is Jeremy's final choice to take on the island?

"To remind me of OFS, I'd take a brooch by Wolf and Moon. Pretty well every woman I know has received a piece of hers from me. When Emily Marston set up the shop for us, her work was not known. Now her jewellery is selling all over the country. We are proud to have helped with her professional development. Another possibility would be the neon light in the entrance. Mary Branson and Jono Retallick made it based on a project with people sleeping rough. It would be great to light up the island."

I pointed out that there may not be electricity on Oxtopia unless some of the scientists have managed to build a generator. Jeremy said "My dad was important in my life and so the card case matters to me but I met Kirsten when I was eighteen. If she can't come with me to Oxtopia, I can't leave without *Fish on a Bicycle*."

Jeremy Spafford

Born: 1959

Occupation: Director OFS

Castaway Items: Darren Greenhow's *Fish on a Bicycle*; 18th-century metal card case engraved with the name of Father Henry Garnet and made to commemorate him

Original OLE Interview: November 2015

Arts at the Old Fire Station is a registered charity and relies on the public buying tickets for shows and gifts from their shop. They welcome donations to help them support homeless people and emerging artists. www.oldfirestation.org.uk

Castaway 3:12
Katie Read

Dynamic theatre director and publicist Katie Read is only thirty-seven, but she accumulated an impressive record of successful theatre productions. She can even boast of assisting Harold Pinter direct his last production and was once assistant director to Sir Trevor Nunn on Tom Stoppard's trilogy, The Coast of Utopia.

Although those experiences are precious to her, her mind is now fixed on her latest venture The Saturday Matinee Company. Having worked at the National Theatre she knows how theatre is easily accessible to the comfortably off, but not on the agenda for those who struggle to make ends meet. The idea behind her no frills theatre company is to put on high quality productions using new and exciting plays at a price anyone can afford. As Katie explained: "When I put on *Connie's Colander* at The Old Fire Station, tickets were priced at 'what you think it is worth and what you can afford', payable after the show." I saw the company's first production Collider and it was indeed first class drama and they played to full houses.

Katie and her young family live in Woodstock where she is best known for directing the town's 2014 Passion Play which made an indelible impression on all who saw it. So where did her passion for theatre come from?

"I was born in Chatham. My father Richard Read was a Hydrographer in the Navy. He wasn't present at my birth as he was at sea a great deal in those days [the dockyards closed later in 1984]. I was breech and my mother Nikki, who now lives in Oxford, likes to say that I have been difficult ever since!"

"When I was three months old my father was mostly working on ships out of Plymouth so my parents moved to Tavistock. Between the ages of five and seven and a half, with my three sisters, Sally, Lizzie and Anna, I enjoyed a special time together in Mississippi, USA when my father was posted there. After school we could walk to the beach and in the holidays my parents hired a camper van and we toured the States. We have wonderful photo albums of those trips and I got into the habit of writing diaries. My diary has to be one of the possibilities for Oxtopia."

When her family returned to England Katie's parents bought a house in Tavistock and like many children of fathers in the services, Katie and her sisters went to boarding school. St Josephs in Launceston in Cornwall was a Roman Catholic school for girls. Katie said, "The school nurtured my love of books. My taste was

for the Brontës and anything to do with King Arthur, poetry and particularly the Romantic poets."

A passion for theatre

"I was a serious student and by the time I won a scholarship to the sixth form at Taunton School, I had developed a passion for theatre. I played Medea in a school production and was given the opportunity to direct plays and I quickly set my heart on a career in the theatre. I have particular happy memories of those two years. I loved English literature too and from then on they were complementary threads in my life, theatre and books. I'm lucky that I have been able to use both in my career."

That was clear from Katie's choice of degree. She read English and Theatre Studies at Leeds but theatre studies gradually had the upper hand. She said,

"I had it in mind to apply to the London Academy of Music and Dramatic Art (LAMDA) to train as an actor after my degree but when I was given the opportunity to study theatre directing at Drama Studio London as well, I took that instead. My friends were cross with me but I observed that actors have to be vulnerable, completely open and lacking in self-consciousness. Directing requires emotional intelligence but allows a little distance: like being behind the camera instead of in front of it. I liked thinking of how the space worked and finding the natural rhythms of a piece. And I love working in technical detail with actors on text."

A well-known fact about any work in the theatre is that until you become a household name it doesn't pay well and the cost of living in London is expensive. So Katie's story is one of being adaptable in order to earn a living.

"In 2000, I set up a company called Hands on Theatre and we played to audiences in Drayton Manor Pub in Ealing. There was no funding so we all had jobs around rehearsals. I had taken a morning cleaning job with a rich family in Bond Street. They paid me well and that income enabled me to support myself while directing Hands on Theatre's first productions. We produced *Blue Remembered Hills* and *The Libertine*, the latter play was set in cabaret style in a pub and it was awarded Critics' Choice in *Time Out*," Katie added.

Following the success of that summer's season of plays, Katie and her colleagues discussed how to use the proceeds.

"We could pay ourselves or use it to rent a space nearer the centre of London. That is what we chose to do. We rented space in Battersea Arts Centre, I felt that *Blue Remembered Hills* was the better production so we repeated it. We had real bark on the floor and had the characters running around the audience. One of the actors had a friend who was a lighting technician at the National Theatre and he arranged for equipment that projected clouds."

"Theatre director Tom Morris [then the artistic director of the BAC who went on to win awards for his Broadway production of War Horse] phoned me and said 'I went to see your show. It was very special. I want you to come and see me.' So I met him and he said 'I want *The Libertine* for my *Time Out* Critic's Choice season in the Studio Theatre.'"

"I told him that our production had worked well in a pub setting but I didn't think it would work in a studio. There was Tom offering me this amazing opportunity and I was saying 'No'! He persuaded me but it didn't do as well as it had in Ealing so I like to remind myself that my instinct was right," Katie added.

However, the production did lead to the opportunity to assist Mick Gordon directing *The Walls* by Colin Teevan and from that to being awarded the Bull Dog Princep Bursary to spend a year as Trainee Director in Residence at The National Theatre Studio.

Theatre: in the thick of it

"I enjoyed the mentorship of Paul Miller and I shared a flat on the Lambeth Walk with actor Nicholas Tennant. I was only twenty-four and already in the thick of it. In retrospect I was too shy and too young to really make the most of it."

"After the bursary, I went straight on to work with Trevor Nunn on *The Coast of Utopia* by Tom Stoppard and during this nine month contract, one of the lead actors, Simon Day, asked me to direct his new version of Turgenev's *The Country Doctor* as a platform production for three nights before the main show on the Olivier stage. It was also during this time that I formed a close working relationship with David Bolger. He was the Artistic Director of his own company, Cois Ceim, an Irish theatre company in Dublin and I went on to spend a great deal of time there working with him. In 2005, our production of *Chamber Made* set in a hotel room won us a Fringe First Award at the Edinburgh Festival.

"I was balancing assisting people like Terry Johnson at the Royal Court with putting on my own shows at fringe venues and teaching at drama schools such as Arts Ed."

"I was young and appeared to be doing really well but it was a struggle financially to live in London and it got to the point that I had to move back with my mother to Oxford! It was a hard thing to accept then and really brought home to me that thus far, I had sacrificed a more traditional and more comfortable career path in order to pursue my passion."

Katie took a break to save some money by doing a data entry temping job for Oxfordshire County Council. It was while she sat at the computer there that she received an email from a West End producer she'd only met a few months previously. Katie was being offered a lifetime opportunity to work with Harold Pinter on what was to be the last play he directed before his death in 2008.

Enter Harold Pinter

"I couldn't believe what I was reading. I managed to get myself living in London again and I remember going to meet Harold for the first time in Holland Park. I wasn't as vocal or as strong then [in 2004] as I am now. Standing on the doorstep,

I made a resolution. I told myself there is no time for shyness or muttering; I mustn't be too in awe. I let my voice come out and be confident...and so I began working with Harold Pinter."

Katie was hired to assist Harold in directing a production at the Comedy Theatre of Simon Gray's *The Old Masters*.

"The rehearsals were wonderful. Harold was incredibly generous. He involved the understudies from day one. The main rehearsals were from 1pm to 6pm so I could rehearse with the understudies all morning. It was a process the understudies really appreciated and felt included. In my contract I had to direct the main rehearsal on two days when Harold was away. Harold said to the cast, 'I am going to leave you in the very capable hands of this young lady'."

Katie continued, "Turning to me he said, 'If you change it, I'll only be intrigued'. When he left me the lead actors just sat down and talked to each other and ignored me. I had to earn my spurs. I was fortunate because in one of my regular trawls of bookshops in Oxford I had found a copy of an old book which was about that particular time in the Art World. It included quotes from Old Masters authorities Bernard Berenson and Joseph Duveen [about 'art' and 'commerce']. I had it with me at that rehearsal. I opened it and took it over to show the actors. They were fascinated by it. Once we'd had a good look, I said simply, 'Okay shall we go from page 71 of the script?' and we did!

"That evening, I walked out on a high and I telephoned my dad. He said, 'You sound just like I did the first time I successfully brought my ship alongside!'"

"I felt close to Harold and he gave me a lot of time. He was generous in asking for my opinion for which I'll always be grateful. He insisted I assist Lindsay Posner directing *The Birthday Party* next and it was a real treat to work on one of his actual plays while we were still in contact.

Then I directed *The Room* with Henry Woolf at the Pinter Festival at Leeds University. It was a great time in my life. The signed volume of limited edition poems by Harold that he gave to the cast and company of *The Old Masters*, has to be a nostalgic possibility for your mythical island Oxtopia," she said to me.

Woodstock passion play

In 2005, Katie met her future partner Peter Morgan in The Gardeners Arms in Oxford. At the same time, she was looking for an occupation that allowed her some financial stability in between theatre jobs so that she didn't have to resort to temping or waitressing all the time.

"I sought an occupation that could give me financial stability and the possibility of a family life. So I set up Read Media and got a retainer contract promoting publisher How To Books and built the company from there. Books have always played an important part in my life and I certainly can't go to Oxtopia without a collection of my favourite ones.

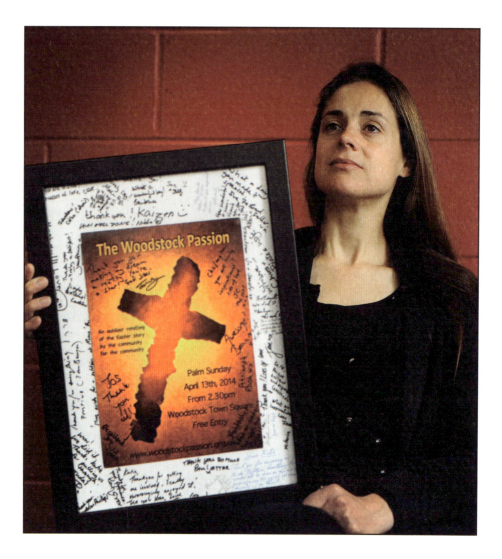

"Peter is a planning consultant in the private sector. When I became pregnant with our son Theo in 2008, we decided to settle here in Oxford and for a while I focussed solely on my work within the publicity company which I still enjoy successfully managing today."

Peter and Katie bought a house in Woodstock and have since had a daughter Sasha.

"I got to know Clare Haynes who is curate of St Mary's Woodstock. She asked me if I would direct the town Passion Play in 2014. It had a cast of around forty and over 1,000 people came to watch it on the day. We 'crucified' Jesus in the Town Square and processed the body to the Museum. All the onlookers everywhere fell into complete silence at this point, it was very moving. The rehearsal process and the performance itself created such a wonderful sense of community, crossing age, gender and even religion as members of our company were Hindu, Muslim, agnostic or even atheist. Another possibility for the island has to be this poster signed by all the cast. It was such a memorable experience and reminded me that I had to somehow fit theatre into my life again.

"My son Theo watched me in rehearsals and I remember thinking how important it is for our children to see us at our best, doing the thing we love."

The Saturday Matinee Company

By this time Katie had got to know the actor Amy Enticknap and through her the actor and writer Gaye Poole. She talked to them about her latest idea and together they combined their talents, experience, passion and complementary personalities and formed The Saturday Matinee Company.

"Jeremy Spafford, [director of The Old Fire Station and fellow Castaway], liked the concept of no thrills, high quality productions at a price affordable to someone walking in off the street and he was very supportive. He later admitted though that he was happily surprised that all three productions in January sold out!"

At the core of the company is a standard format of new plays of one hour in length performed at Saturday lunchtimes. The plays address big questions relevant to society. Early this year I watched their first production *Collider* by Shaun McCarthy. The scenario was that the biggest scientific experiment in history, the Large Hadron Collider is about to be switched on. Scientists are confident it will prove that the universe began with a big bang; religious creationists fear it will create a black hole and destroy the world. Science and religion (and burlesque) are about to collide.

We had come to the moment when I had to ask if she could only take one thing what it would be. She said. "I can't go without my running shoes. I always have to run. It's how I relax." But then she added "Oh and I couldn't be without my books and my diary either..."

Katie Read

Born: 1978

Occupation: Theatre director and publicist

Castaway Items: running shoes, dairy and books

Original OLE Interview: June 2015

If you think you can contribute to its future development through sponsorship please contact Katie, Amy or Gaye via their website www.Satmatco.com

Legs Larry Smith

Graphic artist and writer as well as a musician, "Legs" Larry Smith is up there with rock'n'roll royalty. As tuba player turned drummer for the quintessentially English Bonzo Dog Doo-Dah Band, he was befriended by The Beatles, and George Harrison even wrote a song about him: *His Name Is Legs (Ladies and Gentlemen).*

And that's not all: "Legs" Larry also accompanied Elton John and Eric Clapton on tours of the States often tap dancing in a tutu with half-a-dozen chorus girls. Today he can count Stephen Fry as one of the band's big fans. Somehow Larry is both the artist and the art but not everything in his life has gone smoothly for this Oxford-born muso.

"I was born at the old Radcliffe Infirmary," Larry began, "my father Alec was born in Yorkshire and my mother Olive in Lancashire. Alec was a bricklayer and headed south looking for work. They settled in Ferry Road, New Marston but Alec worked for a while in Brighton."

"It must have been like discovering Eldorado because my father wrote to his parents suggesting they move there. The whole family took his advice and moved to nearby Shoreham. We had holidays in Brighton and in Manchester where my mother's family lived. The contrast was stark. I remember the gleaming doorsteps polished to perfection by Manchester housewives in defiance of the soot and grime that covered everything."

Larry was an only child but had a regular companion – a dog called Trixie. He loved walking near the Cherwell and thought the world was greener and the fish more plentiful on the University Parks side of the river. That is why he chose to have his photo-shoot on the High Bridge. He said, "I used to leap over the edge of the bridge and land in the park which you weren't supposed to do. My rebellion started early."

Larry's education at the local primary school was interrupted when, aged nine and a half, he contracted Rheumatic Fever.

"I was admitted to the Radcliffe Infirmary and sent to convalesce in the Savanake Forest in Wiltshire. There were no opportunities for lessons or learning in hospital so I relieved the tedium by drawing blobby people, cartoon-like sketches. I missed a whole year of school and consequently failed my eleven plus."

The potential of art

"I was sent to Northway Estate Secondary Modern School and was lucky to have an inspirational art teacher named Grahame Miller, who recognised that I had potential. Mr Miller took me and fellow student David Mitchell to London, to the Tate Gallery and to the Curzon cinema to see an art house film of Picasso painting directly to camera on glass. I was inspired and started to win art prizes. Grahame approached my parents, suggesting I apply to art school. I put a portfolio together and won a place at the Oxford School of Art on the site of Oxford Brookes University.

"The various courses gave me good grounding in art but, when contemporary artists from London visited us, I concluded that the teachers were stuck in a previous era and London was where I had to be. I transferred to Central St Martins and studied there for three years eventually receiving a National Diploma in Design."

Larry particularly liked problem solving and graphic design and was attracted to the world of advertising, which in the 1960s was particularly innovative and creative. The capital of the advertising world was across the Atlantic.

Three goofy guys in New York

"In my penultimate year, with two other guys and my portfolio I headed for New York. If you were British in New York in 1964 you were considered princes. The Beatles were gods. Taxi drivers leant out of their cab windows and shouted 'You guys are great.' We looked different, (English) and had an aura of irresponsibility. Girls followed us in the streets, eventually plucking up courage to approach us. I tried telling them we were nothing to do with rock'n'roll and that we were merely art students from London England, but they wouldn't believe it. 'Wow London England' they gasped and asked for our autographs."

They took their design portfolios to a famous advertising agency McCann Erickson. Larry said,

"They sent us to an innovative sister company called McCann Marshal who gave us six weeks work. I worked on a logo design for 'Tab', a soft drink. They took us to endless lunches to show off three groovy English guys."

Larry added, "An idea for my castaway object is the type rule given me in the Time Life building by Bill Free – the head of the agency. The pleasure and real affection I have for this rare piece of designer's steel is quite something – for one thing, I haven't actually lost it. I can defend myself and hack my way through the jungle. Also, it has lots of tiny grooves– for when I feel like being groovy."

The grooviness obviously rubbed off because the three young art students were introduced to Peter Max. With his friend Tom Daly, Peter Max (nee Peter Max Finkelstein), the German-born American illustrator and graphic artist, had started a small Manhattan arts studio known as The Daly & Max Studio where they were making a name for themselves in psychedelic art. Larry said,

"Peter's innovative work was everywhere on buses and on the metro. After our six week's work we headed for Villa Park, Chicago to visit my aunt Betty who had married a GI. In the Midwest too, the local girls thought us 'glamorous pop-stars' and there were always a couple hanging around my aunt's house, leaning over the Wilson picket fence. We went to a Drive-in, raced a GTO and 'hung out' at a cool new MacDonald's where we ordered endless Big Macs for 39 cents. The chain was just beginning to take off in the States. Charles C. Cooper the manager, gave me his 'degree' certificate, his 'Batchelor of Hamburgerology' would you believe, and I still have it."

They headed back to New York. When the time came to leave the USA Peter Max turned up, in his canary yellow convertible Volkswagen to drive them to the airport.

"It was a crazy holiday. I rang the airport to check on our Air Lingus student flight to be told it had left three hours ago. We had no money and in those days no credit cards. We were telling the story to a hysterical Peter when around the corner came an oriental gentleman, extremely 'posh' and suffering from an English education. He was carrying a bottle of Jack Daniels. He approached us and said 'Excuse me, are you Liverpudlians?' We said: 'NO, NO, NO, we're definitely not (we'd had quite enough of 'adoring recognition') – we're from London and have spent all our money, missed our flights and have no idea how to get back to England."

 "'Don't worry,' he said, blowing bubbles, 'Come with me.' We all bundled into Peter's car and headed off for Kennedy Airport swigging his Jack Daniels and beginning to care less and less about the flight home. He said 'Which airline?' Then answered his own question. 'You're British so you should really fly BOAC.' This total stranger went up to the counter and asked for three tickets 'to London England, please', produced a credit card and paid for our flights home. We later on discovered he was the owner of the Five Spot Jazz Club and refunded him."

Birth of the Bonzos

McCann-Marshall offered Larry a job once he had finished his final year at college and he had every intention of returning to New York. But in the meantime he had met Vivian Stanshall and that changed everything.

"Vivian was a fellow student and regarded as a cool dude. He stood out with his dandified manner and bright red hair. He was serious about 'Bonzo' and was already forming the band and some months later, asked me to join as the tuba player. Alas, I really fancied the drums. As a delinquent I'd beat out rhythms with my mum's knitting needles on her coffee table. I borrowed his B flat tuba, sat on my Mother's carpet (blowing, huffing and puffing) and by the end of a week had managed to make an acceptable sound. I returned to London and passed my second audition. The Bonzo Dog Doo-Dah Band began to play twice a week in pubs."

When Larry reached the end of his graphic design course he had the opportunity to head up an Italian design team in Milan.

"I didn't take that either because queues formed whenever we played so Kenny Ball's manager Reg Tracey came to watch us. In his best Essex manner he said 'Hello boys. I'll make you rich and famous.' Ho, ho. We made our TV debut in February 1966, performing *Won't You Come Home Bill Bailey* on the BBC's children's programme Blue Peter.

"Our first sight of the Beatles was at EMI's Abbey Road studio where both bands were recording. Such was the power of their image that we joined the cleaning ladies, secretaries and maintenance men on the stairs to watch as Lennon's black Rolls Royce turned up. They jumped out with their suits and their smiles – 'Hullo, Hullo, Hullo, Hullo –' they said and raced off to Studio A.

"In 1967, we were booked on a six week tour of northern cabaret clubs. Admission was free. For the price of a couple of beers you could see a line-up of top variety acts which meant that the clubs were packed with incredible audiences out for a good time. Staying at a venue for a whole week meant we could create a show and rehearse new songs during the day.

"Then came the offer from Paul McCartney to take part in the Beatles film The *Magical Mystery Tour*. We feigned illness, left the cabaret club and headed south. Paul wanted us to play a backing band in a Soho strip joint and that's exactly what we did. Afterwards there was a wonderful rap party at the Royal Lancaster Hotel. Everyone came in fancy dress. Paul and Jane Asher dressed as pearly king and queen. Lennon was toughing it out as a rocker in leathers. George Martin, their producer arrived with his wife as the Duke of Edinburgh and the Queen and when they arrived they were breathtakingly real – they looked so regal."

On Boxing Day 1967, the fledgling ITV launched a ground-breaking show called *Do Not Adjust Your Set*. The show took its name from the message, which was displayed when there was a problem with transmission (often in those days). Starring the future Pythons, it acquired cult status and ran till May 1969. The Bonzos played in each programme with Larry playing drums, singing in the band and tap-dancing in a tutu. In 1968 the band had a hit with *I'm The Urban Spaceman* produced by Paul McCartney and Gus Dudgeon under the collective pseudonym Apollo C. Vermouth.

The Bonzos played their final gig in January 1970 although it was not quite final because they reconvened a couple of times, sadly without Vivian ["Viv got ill with a combination of Valium and alcohol"].

Song for George – song for Larry

The Beatles had become fans of the group. "Around that time I got to know George Harrison's PA, Terry Doran, Terry and I were becoming good friends, hanging out at The Marquee club. Terry told George 'You've got to meet Larry.' We had an official meeting lined up when he was recording *My Sweet Lord* over at Trident Studios.

A couple of months later he telephoned and invited me over to Friar Park for dinner. I figured he was lining up a sneaky surprise. He breezed into the grand hall, nodded hello and seated himself at the piano. There he was at his Steinway with a Tiffany lamp and the Wurlitzer casting a warm glow over proceedings when I realised that the song he was playing was about me! Oh, Lordy. [It was *His Name Is Legs (Ladies and Gentlemen)* which appeared later on Harrison's 1975 solo album *Extra Texture (Read All About It)*]. We just clicked and became closer than close. He called me The King of La di Da."

That was how Larry became a close friend of George Harrison. After the Beatles broke up Larry designed the cover for George's *Gone Troppo* album (1982). "We did lots of incredible things together. I went with George to an Ayurvedic retreat in Boston for ten days where we met Mo Austin, the head of Warner Brothers. The retreat was led by the now famous Depak Chopra. He said 'You have to find the place inside yourself where nothing is impossible.' I learned transcendental meditation and enjoyed blissful hot sesame oil massages (Panchakarma)."

"I miss George" muses Larry, "he had such warmth and a great sense of humour. There was one favour I wanted to return. I wrote a song about him and called it *Oh Keoki*. Keoki is George in Hawaiian. We had great times there."

Enter Elton

"Gus Dudgeon [Elton John's producer] rang to ask me to tap dance to Elton's song *I think I'm Going To Kill Myself*." For me, the technical side of tap dancing is merely drumming with your feet." The track appeared on the album *Honky Chateau* (1972) after which Elton asked Larry to accompany him on a tour of the USA.

"I flew out first-class and Elton and I eventually met in a huge gymnasium somewhere in the Mid-West. We entered from different sides of the arena and slowly strode into the middle – meeting like two camp gunfighters in a western. The tour was magical. Elton and I did a song and dance routine to *Singin' in the Rain* – which went down a storm – *A Clockwork Orange*, had made the soundtrack song 'hip'. After each show we looked for an Indian restaurant. In those days, there didn't seem to be any apart from in New York and maybe LA."

His LA highlight was tea with Mae West (Elton, John Reed, Elton's long-time partner and manager, and aspiring actor John Lazar in 1972 also joined Larry).

"I arrived for tea at three. Her black-tie butler opened the door and bid us welcome and we were reverently shown into a 'breath-taking world of white'.

The stillness of the room, coupled with the acrid bouquet of orchids, gave it the air of an undertaker's chapel of repose – a mortuary. We were nervously staring at each other in whispers. Five, ten silly minutes drifted by then Chan, the butler, reappeared saying 'Gentlemen – Miss West.'"

"Staring straight ahead through giant 'panda' eyes with lashes caked in thick black clumps of make-up, and platinum blonde hair piled to within an inch of the chandelier, she glided among us, passing through us, an arm raised in greeting like the Statue of Liberty, and broke the ice with: 'Ummm...wall to wall men – I like it!'"

Larry painted a picture of Mae West and on the island it would remind him of that heady time.

Enter Eric

Two years later Larry returned to the USA on tour with Eric Clapton.

"I opened, did a few funnies and then announced Eric. Then, halfway through the show, when Eric was about to do one of his blistering solos, I rushed out with a toy plastic guitar and mimed his solo. I smashed it up and jumped on it – 'doing a Pete Townsend' jumped on a tap-dancing board and danced my ass off! It went down amazingly well with the audience. For the final show the roadies gave me a superb new Jumbo acoustic guitar to smash. I said 'Guys this is a beautiful guitar: I can't smash this. 'Yes you can'' they said. 'We loved your stuff and it's the last night.' When the magic moment came to smash it – all the roadies rushed onstage, lifted me aloft and wrapped me up with gaffer tape. There I was, bound up like an Egyptian mummy when Pete Townsend came onto the stage picked up the guitar and smashed it."

Larry said "Doh! It was all good clean fun." But by this time not everything about touring was as fun and healthy.

Beating the demons

"I spent the next thirty years in pubs and bars, with a notebook and a pencil – convincing myself that I was working. I was offered lots of opportunities but generally always messed them up at the last minute. Brian Forbes invited me to lunch at the Café Royal saying 'You'll make a great DJ. You'll be perfect on Capital Radio.' When it came to the audition I got horribly drunk and rang and cancelled."

It took a long time but family life helped him beat the demons of his rock and roll life style. Larry said,

"I moved to my Oxfordshire village in 1989 and became friends with Sylvia Larkin Smith. I married her daughter, Sarah twelve years ago. Having children has focussed me. We have eleven-year-old twins Rebecca Daisy and Delphie Rose. Alcohol was the monkey on my back and I've finally sent that particular monkey to join the troupe on Gibraltar. I haven't had a drink in eleven years and I'm somewhat proud of that. Now, work is the thing. I start work around five every morning in my garden studio – my 'Shedio'. I've got all this damned creativity to release, a portfolio of promise and pleasure. It's been like a rebirth. I've gone back to the beginning – to good old art. When I write music I tend to think visually to set a scene. Art helps.

In the noughties there have been several Bonzo reunions and further ones can never be ruled out. Speaking of which when I pressed Larry on what is his final choice to take to Oxtopia would be, it was the type measure.

Legs Larry Smith

Born: 1944

Occupation: Drummer, tap dancer, graphic artist

Castaway Items: type rule (for graphic designers) and Larry's picture of Mae West

Original OLE Interview: January 2015

Fiona Carnarvon

Not many people can boast a view of four counties from their house, but proud home owner Lady Carnarvon can from her Jacobean style Highclere Castle near Newbury. You might know it better as *Downton Abbey*.

Highclere Castle had attracted film and TV production companies before in the TV series *Jeeves and Wooster*, and the Heath Ledger movie *The Four Feathers*. But *Downton Abbey* became the most widely watched television drama – the last season of the upstairs/downstairs family saga had a huge following in China. All of this means Highclere Castle has become one of the best known stately homes in the world.

It seems that no one was more surprised at the success of the ITV series than Lady Carnarvon, wife to the 8th Earl of Carnarvon. She said, "We hoped at best that it might be like *Brideshead Revisited* a TV series followed by a film." And it turns out the real life stories within the walls of Highclere are as colourful as those of Julian Fellowes' fiction.

She was born Fiona Aitken in London, the eldest of six daughters of Ronnie and Frances Aitken.

"I enjoyed a privileged childhood with a wonderful mother and a nanny who is still part of the family. Our grandparents lived just around the corner. There were walks in St James Park and much more."

Fiona's father worked in the city but they left London to holiday in Polzeath in Cornwall every summer. "It was very much an outdoors type of holiday with football on the beach, rock climbing, shrimping and lots of walking. Loads of friends would come down and stay. But it wasn't as fashionable a place as it is now. "

I asked about her education.

"My first school was unusual. Hampshire School was run by the mother and sister of actress Susan Hampshire. I remember it as happy place with lots of dancing. It was lovely to welcome Susan here recently for a fundraising event for a dyslexia charity."

Fiona described her secondary education at St Paul's Girls School.

"All the teachers were excellent. They instilled confidence in us to read and discuss what we had read. I was already a bookworm. I had several inspirational English teachers, Mrs Hall and Miss Gough. Thanks to them I have an abiding love of the metaphysical poets. There was lots of Shakespeare and speaking in cadence. My father wanted us to be good at languages. He particularly loves Schiller and Goethe. I took English, History and German at 'A' level."

Fiona went on to explain that while her French speaking was quite good she felt her German could do with improving so, after 'A' levels, she took a gap year in Germany working in a clothing factory.

A student in Scotland

It must have helped as 1984 saw Fiona heading for St Andrews University where she read English and German, as well as learning to fish and going on hikes.

I wondered why she had chosen to go to university in Scotland?

"My grandfather was a keen and good golfer and he loved St Andrews. My father's family is Scottish so I saw it as an opportunity to explore that beautiful part of Great Britain. In those days St Andrews was completely unspoiled. It had one coffee shop, one supermarket, a chemist, a fish and chip shop and a shop which sold watercolours. I made a huge number of wonderful friends there.

"During most holidays, I worked as a temp to pay back what I'd overspent during term time. Those experiences gave me an insight into different kinds of work opportunities. I decided I wanted to be a management consultant but realised I needed a particular skill. I thought either a qualification in law or accountancy would make me employable. I qualified as a chartered accountant with Coopers and Lybrand."

Her love of books led Fiona to try her hand at writing non-fiction. Surprisingly she said the experience has helped her with her books.

"When you are confronted with an idea, you need to organise your thoughts, do research and analyse the results. You have to try to assess what is accurate and then present your statement of accounts. For both accountancy and for my books, you have to have the reader in mind."

It was also through a book that she met the eighth Earl, George 'Geordie' Herbert. They were seated next to one another at a charity dinner in 1996. Geordie was coping with the end of his short-lived first marriage, which had produced a daughter, Saoirse, and a son George who will eventually become the ninth Earl of Carnarvon. Fiona said,

"We discovered we had a mutual interest in First World War poetry. Afterwards he sent me a book of poetry, which I still have. I thanked him and we soon realised we also shared so many interests including a love of reading, tennis, the countryside and mutual friends."

Highclere becomes home

So it was perhaps not surprising that they married in February 1999. I asked if she had worried about what she would be taking on.

"I didn't really think about it at the time. Geordie's grandfather had lived until he was ninety and I assumed his father would be around for decades so, it was a shock when he died just two years after our marriage. I was happy and lucky that I had got to know him during that time because Geordie is so similar to his father."

Her father in law, Henry Herbert, the 7th Earl of Carnarvon, loved horse racing and became manager to the Queen. She was a frequent visitor to Highclere until his death in 2001. Fiona said,

"When he died I didn't think about how it would change our lives only about trying to comfort his grieving son.

For the past eleven years she has managed the house which has been in the Carnarvon family since 1679. The 8th Earl concentrates mostly on the estate. Lady Carnarvon said,

"I learn more each day from the people I'm working with. Diana, the housekeeper, has been here for over twenty-five years, and some of the others have been here for fifty years. I'm not trying to dictate to them but, in the end, I am responsible and we're trying to create the income to continue to employ them. The staff completely 'get this' and we work together as a community."

Before *Downton* it was far from easy. As of 2009, repairs needed for the estate were estimated to cost at around £12 million, £1.8 million of which was urgently needed for the castle. Fiona said,

"To be a real home, we needed to undertake a lot of work especially to the bedrooms and bathrooms. I wanted to bring my sisters and their families here often and fill it with warmth and love."

Then there are the friends they regularly entertain. One of their oldest friends is the writer Julian Fellows.

"After he'd written Gosford Park, Julian tried to get it filmed here in 2001 but we accepted it when the director, Robert Altman, chose to set the movie elsewhere."

Writing the real *Downton* stories

The real stories of Highclere are every bit as colourful as Julian Fellow's fiction.

"He particularly likes writing about the Edwardian era. Once I realised they would plunge into a second series, I threw myself into writing a real historical book and called it *Lady Almina and the Real Downton Abbey*." said Fiona. "Almina was the illegitimate daughter of the banking tycoon, Alfred de Rothschild, who married

the fifth Earl and whose wealth was very useful in 1895. It was agreat opportunity to reach a big audience and the book has been sold in over twenty countries.

In the Morning Room where we were sitting hangs a portrait of a pale and slender woman, with a twenties bob, wearing an elegant white silk dress. She was the American-born Lady Catherine, Geordie's grandmother, who divorced the sixth Earl of Carnarvon, the philandering Porchey, and was the subject of Fiona Carnarvon's second book, *Lady Catherine, and the Real Downton Abbey*.

"I concentrated on researching the twenties and thirties. History matters. The story of the Wall Street Crash and all the economic struggles and hardship for many in the thirties leading to the success of the Labour Party after the Second World War and the introduction of the welfare state has relevance today."

I asked what books are likely to come next.

"Before 1679, Highclere was the home of the Bishops of Winchester from the eighth century. I want to write about that period."

That should be of interest locally because the medieval bishops of Winchester were hugely significant to Oxford particularly William of Wykeham who founded New College Oxford and New College School in 1379. Fiona also writes a blog and has compiled a cookery book with anecdotes and recipes from the last 200 years.

"I enjoy writing my blog and you learn a lot from the response you get. People are interested in the traditional recipes we have used at different times. I like trying them out with our chef. But I have an ambition to write about the gardens designed by Capability Brown and about Charles Barry the architect of the house. Not forgetting Egypt. I wrote about George Herbert the 5th Earl in *Egypt at Highclere: The Discovery of Tutankhamun*. He was not just an enthusiastic photographer but a respected professional. He became a pioneer of colour photography and was asked to be President of the Camera Club in 1916. That is another book waiting to be written."

Last year Fiona Carnavon and her husband opened the exhibition Discovering Tutankhamun at the Ashmolean. It was the 5th earl as an enthusiastic amateur Egyptologist who sponsored the excavation of nobles' tombs in Thebes in 1907 and accompanied Howard Carter during the discovery of the young Pharaoh's tomb in 1922.

Thanks to the *Downton* effect – with visitor numbers rocketing – the financial future of Highclere as a home to the Carnarvons looks safe.

As for her castaway art objects and books, Fiona replied, "It has to be books and the war poets and Metaphysical poets are not enough – I would like to take the Highclere Library. That should keep me occupied and can I have lots of paper and pens on some of the shelves?"

Her fellow Oxtopians will appreciate Fiona's arrival on the island for both her company and the library she brings with her. She had made it her ambition to make Highclere a home full of warmth, love and friendship and that would be a fitting ambition for Oxtopia too.

Fiona Carnavon

Born: 1963

Occupation: Wife of the 8th Earl of Carnarvon, owner of Highclere House

Castaway Items: Highclere Library

Original OLE Interview: February 2015

Castaway 3:15
Mark Davies

Mark J. Davies talked to me on his narrowboat home, Bill the Lizard, moored by the towpath on the Oxford Canal which he describes as 'a hidden gem'. Moving there in 1992 changed his life and set him on his career as a local historian and author of six books about Oxford.

For Mark life began in Lyndhurst in the New Forest. By coincidence Alice Liddell, the inspiration for Alice in Wonderland is buried in that town. Although his sojourn there was brief the character of Alice has significance in Mark's life today. On his narrowboat he wrote Alice in Waterland.

"My father, John Glyn Davies, who preferred to be known as Glyn, was born in South Wales but his work as a customs officer meant I had a peripatetic childhood. We moved from Southampton to Seaford to Porthcawl and to Dover twice. Most of my primary school years were spent in Dover. From eleven to fourteen, I attended Bridgend Grammar School. At that time our home was in Porthcawl. My memories of Porthcawl are idyllic because we lived near the beach and had the freedom to roam and play with lots of kids of the same age in a safe environment."

At the age of about nine Mark enjoyed his first writing success when he received a postal order for two shillings and sixpence from The Beano when they published a Mark Davies letter.

"When I was fourteen my father was re-appointed to Dover and so I completed my grammar school education in Dover. I took 'A' levels in French, German and Geography."

His parents were hoping he would pursue a career in law or accountancy but Mark had a mind of his own at an early age.

Angus Wilson and letters of introduction

"My mother Jeanne's background was Scottish and my great uncle Angus Wilson, the author, influenced my life choices. We share a middle name of Johnstone. Uncle Angus sent me postcards from all over the world, which encouraged me to collect stamps and to take an interest in geography. He it was who indirectly inspired my wander lust."

"Instead of going to university after leaving school I headed for the hippy trail. At the time I had no idea that we had family connections there – no-one did – but Angus' influence drew me to India.

"I heard about Ashley Butterfield who organised journeys to Asia. He arranged all travel by public transport from here to India and accommodation along the way for groups of travellers. I worked for a while to raise the money to pay Ashley for the trip out and to save what seems like not much money today to live there for six months. Currency restrictions were enforced at the time, so you pretty much had to take whatever you needed with you, and spread your spending so as to have enough to get home again!"

"Angus gave me a letter of introduction. In Delhi I met the daughter of Ruth Prawer Jhabvala, the author of Heat and Dust. She drove me around Delhi and laughed because it was not only unusual for a woman to be driving in Delhi in 1975 and to have a white man in the passenger seat really turned heads."

"In Bharatpur in Rajastan, I handed over Angus' card to the Maharaja who had no hesitation in inviting me to dinner in his palace. Much later on he asked me 'Who exactly is this Angus Wilson?' He had provided hospitality even though he hadn't remembered my uncle! Subsequently I kept in touch with his son for many years. I'd acquired a taste for India which stayed with me."

On his homecoming, it wasn't law or accountancy to keep his parents happy but music that beckoned.

"I caught up with old friends, who were in a band called Back Van Nasty. We won a competition which paid for time in a recording studio and went in search of the bright lights of London, ten of us sharing a house in Acton. To begin with I managed the group and wrote our lyrics. We enjoyed some success and employed professional management but it didn't work out and the band imploded.

"To pay my way I found work with a company called Saccone and Speed who imported wines and developed knowledge about and a taste for wine and that experience eventually brought me to Oxfordshire."

By 1979, Mark's itchy feet were longing to travel again.

"My older sister, Penny was living in Namibia and I prearranged the travel to Jo'burg but when I reached Windhoek I was diagnosed with malaria. To return I hitchhiked to Nairobi, via South Africa, Zimbabwe, Malawi and Tanzania. I rarely had to wait long by the road. People were hospitable. I remember persuading Nadine Gordimer and her husband to drive me out of Johannesburg. I had turned up out of the blue with another of Angus Wilson's effective cards of introduction, and she felt obliged. Pretty cheeky really – and of Angus too, now that I think of it."

In 1981, Mark decided to read for a degree in geography at Middlesex Polytechnic, firstly at Hendon, then Enfield. But the settled life was not to last long. He abandoned his studies, worked for six months to afford to travel to India again and, from there crossed Asia to Thailand and Indonesia and finally to Australia and New Zealand – a two year journey.

On returning to the UK, Mark realised he needed a proper job and after going back into the wine trade this time in Didcot, volunteered for Oxfam, and later got a permanent job as a fundraiser.

"It was one of few organisations where my travelling experience worked to my advantage. I'd found my niche and worked for Oxfam for the next eighteen years," said Mark.

An Oxfam colleague opened his eyes to the attractions of living on a houseboat.

"I loved the fact that I was surrounded by water and peaceful countryside and yet within five minutes' walk of the city centre."

Oxford Towpath writer

The location of his unusual new home was to catapult him into his writing career specialising in local history.

"In 1997, The Oxford Times ran a science writing competition in collaboration with The Natural History Museum. In 1795–97, an unsung hero, Daniel Harris built Isis Lock, a broad lock to allow Thames barges in and out of the canal terminus at Worcester Street wharves. I wrote a tongue-in-cheek piece about how I used the lock as a rain gauge and won a prize. It gave me a taste for writing. In 1998, I began writing regularly about residential life on the canal for Canal & River Boat magazine."

"Until the 1980s the canal was neglected. That began to change during the nineties and when British Waterways set up a forum for all interested parties, Catherine Robinson [another local writer and editor] I wrote Our Canal in Oxford as one of its tangible elements. I self-published it under the imprint Oxford Towpath Press in 1999 and expanded it to include the River Thames in A Towpath Walk in Oxford (2001)."

The Oxford Canal had become an important part of Mark's life and he showed me a possible castaway work of art: a framed engraving of The Observatory and Printing Office viewed from the canal. Unusually for 18th-century images of Oxford it includes a smoking chimney. Maybe that is because the artist visitor Carl Rundt was German. It captures the dual personality that is a canal representing industry and picturesque countryside, and is featured in four of Mark's books, hence his affection for it.

Mark's historical hero Daniel Harris was prison governor from 1786 until 1809. But he was also a builder, engineer, artist, and architect. As well as supervising the construction work at the prison, his ability to provide an all-in service of design, creation, and labour meant he was in demand for construction projects in the Oxford area including the canal. He completed the canal basin terminus (today's Worcester Street car park) as well as Isis Lock. Mark said,

"My interest in Daniel Harris led me to read records of Oxford prison. It was mostly a tale of human misery. One story particularly caught my imagination. While Harris was governor a certain Giles Covington was executed for murder. The story gripped me and became the subject of my next book The Abingdon Waterturnpike Murder (2003).

The Jericho boatyard saga

Mark described the impact of the closing of Jericho boatyard. "Every four years boats need to be taken out of the water for blacking the hulls in order to keep them free from rust and water tight. Like others along here I used to have my boat serviced at Jericho. British Waterways wanted to sell some properties and they decided to sell the Jericho boatyard but the manner in which they failed to consult has cost us dearly. They arbitrarily closed the whole yard including the repair yard which meant that our nearest boatyard is either on the Thames or beyond the Cherwell, many hours away. Alchemy Boats, which had been renting the site for boat repairs had to leave and the boaters occupied part of the site to maintain the service facility. British Waterways sent in the bailiffs and fenced off the site. The ugly fence has been almost a decade.

"The author Philip Pullman spoke eloquently on the boaters' behalf and he paid for our barrister. The boatyard and the nearby canal provided him with inspiration for his community of 'gyptians', a group of nomadic boat people who appear in the His Dark Materials trilogy. We succeeded in having two unpleasant development plans rejected. In February 2015, a much more enlightened developer the Strategic Iconic Assets Heritage Acquisition Fund (SIAHAF) obtained planning permission for development of the canal side site – but subject to forty-five conditions.

"As well as Philip's books, *Where the Rivers Meet* by John Wayne is a favourite of mine and they are possible books to take to the island of Oxtopia. And I haven't read *The Lord of the Rings* cycle since I was a teenager so that could be something with which to grapple on the island too, given Tolkien's Oxford connections (and Welsh ones)."

The most famous fictional character with an association to Oxford is Alice in Wonderland and Mark wrote about the importance of the local waterways in Alice Liddell's story and in the story Lewis Carroll made up for her while rowing past Port Meadow. Mark called his book *Alice in Waterland* (2010/2012), and that was followed by *Alice's Oxford on Foot* (2014). It is not surprising that he has been involved in The Story Museum's "Alice's Day" since its inception, and now leads regular walks – the only ones endorsed by the Lewis Carroll Society – though relevant parts of Oxford. He also provides commentaries on Thames' cruises operated by Oxford River Cruises and has hosted Mad Hatter's Tea Parties at Christ Church.

What would a towpath traveller choose to take to Oxtopia?.

"I'd like to take Bill the Lizard but if that isn't possible it will have to be this model of it, which was made to order in Zimbabwe by a young guy I met while visiting friends there. I sent him a photo, and this was the impressively to-scale result. But I also like this wooden pencil-box, also made to order at Restore on the Cowley Road."

In the past I have turned down castaways' wishes to take buildings to Oxtopia but since Mark's home is transportable, it was hard to say 'No'. Moreover, the subject of Mark's seventh book is the first Englishman to fly (in a balloon and in Oxford). James Sadler was the entrepreneurial son of an Oxford High Street pastry cook. There has been an element of gypsy restlessness to Mark's life so the knowledge that Bill the Lizard can be untied and glide away like Sadler's hot air balloon is very appealing.

Mark Davies

Born: 1955

Occupation: Author and canal walks guide

Castaway Items: Bill the Lizard (his houseboat); wooden pencil-box, books including Philip Pullman's *His Dark Materials* trilogy, John Wayne's *Where the Rivers Meet* and Tolkien's *The Lord of the Rings*

Original OLE Interview: September 2015

Mark leads canal walks, go to www.oxfordwaterwalks.co.uk

Castaway 3:16
Nancy Hunt

I can officially describe Nancy Hunt as inspirational because she won the Venus 2015 UK Inspirational Woman Award. I am convinced she deserves that description. Her journey has taken her from a tough upbringing in rural Kenya to being Director of The Nasio Trust – a charity whose Early Childhood Development Centres provide a daily meal, pre-primary education and medical care to almost 400 children there.

But it was an incident fifteen years ago in Kenya which changed her life completely. Nancy was faced with a huge challenge to turn her life upside down and leave her successful career in the Thames Valley Police. She faced it with a certain amount of reluctance but once the decision was made, she set about growing the Nasio Trust with a fierce determination.

I usually begin interviews by asking our castaway when and where they were born. This is the first time the castaway could say where she was born but not exactly when she was born.

Nancy explained: "I was born in the village of Musanda near Mumias Town in Western Kenya. The town was named after my paternal grandfather, a tribal chief. The British maintained the tribal institutions for administrative purposes so my father George Mudenyo was the administrative chief. As such he attended the coronation of Queen Elizabeth II and proudly showed us the photographs.

"As chief he was desperate for sons but my mother, Irene, bore him nine daughters before she had four boys. I was their thirteenth child. As a girl I wasn't valued and that is probably why my father failed to register my birth. Some years later, my sister Betty decided that I needed a birth certificate and she registered me.

"She conjured up the date of 10th January 1970 although nobody knew for certain when I was born. I had been named Ishmael after my grandfather. Betty felt that I should have a girl's name and, on the certificate, I am Nancy Ishmael Ndula. A few years ago, I visited my grandfather's grave and discovered that he had died in November 1974. From family stories I had the idea that my mother was pregnant with me when he was dying and that was why she named me after him. So I have the choice of being either five years older or five years younger.

The influence of Irene, her mother

"My mother, Irene, was the daughter of a preacher and regarded as a suitable wife for a chief. She was married when she was only fifteen. As a child she had responsibility for siblings so never received an education and regretted it all her life. Although she was illiterate, she was determined that her girls would be educated.

"My mother was an industrious farmer in the village of Ibinda. Each week she took vegetables to sell in the market in the nearby town of Musanda. From the profits she paid for all her girls to go to school. Market days were exciting ones. She chose one of us to go with her."

Irene set up her stall and then left Nancy to do the selling while she set off to a club for a drink. My mother was hurt when my father married another five wives and neglected her. Drinking was her escape her means of deadening the pain," said Nancy.

"She returned at midday and bought me lunch and lunch contained a rare thing, meat. That alone made me want to go with her to market."

"On the rare occasion that father visited, my mother and he would go into the sitting room and bring out the wind-up gramophone (we had no electricity) and play music and drink tea. A wind-up gramophone is a possibility for the island.

A consequence of her mother's developing alcoholism was that she left the club late and Nancy described their late journey home.

"It was pitch black as we walked the six miles home from the market town. If she saw a rare vehicle in the distance she would hide us in the bushes. She insisted I carry three stones. One in each hand and one on my head in case they were needed to defend us from man or animal. When we arrived home, she would sing drunkenly and throw water on the cooking fire and if my siblings had not eaten they would go hungry. I felt ashamed and sad because I had eaten and they would sleep hungry.

"When it was my turn to be left at home, I often went hungry. Unless you have experienced hunger as a child you can't really know how it feels. We all slept on a mat on the floor, three to a blanket. Sleeping in the middle was best because when your siblings tossed and turned they pulled the blanket off the ones at the end.

"When my mother realised what a waste of her life drinking was, she conquered her addiction," said Nancy. "When I was twelve, my mother arranged for me to go to boarding school in Migori close to the Tanzanian border. It took almost twenty-four hours to get there. At school I experienced the luxury of having a bed to myself. The downside was that I had no visits and no contact with my family and I was lonely.

"Each term my mother gave me the school fees in cash. She folded it in a cloth and tied it around my waist. She told me on no account to loosen or take off any layers of clothing to prevent it from being stolen. It meant the journey was hot and sticky. But I learned to be independent and my school friends became my family. Around this time I first read a book for pleasure – a dog-eared copy of a Danielle Steele novel – a bit of escapism. Another possibility for the island? "

A young women in a developing country . . .

Nancy was able academically so she won a place at a Kenyan University to study education with the ambition of following her sisters and becoming a teacher. It is hard for British teenagers to understand the problems facing young women in developing countries. With her place at university, she was entitled to a government loan. Her immediate priority was to buy her first packet of sanitary towels. Lack of them is one of the greatest obstacles for girls receiving secondary education in Africa and some parts of India. Her intimate understanding of the problem means providing underwear and sanitary protection is one of the priorities for the older girls whom Nasio supports.

She says "Teenage girls are known to sell themselves for risky sex with older men just to be able to buy sanitary towels."

There was one big change to her week while at university. Nancy said,

"Every Sunday throughout my childhood, we dressed in our best clothes even if it was hand-me-downs and went to church. My boarding school was Anglican and a church service was part of every day. As a student I never once went to church. Now I wouldn't want to do without my faith. I draw strength from it when I'm feeling overwhelmed by what I have taken on."

After graduating Nancy worked for a while in a boy's school teaching geography and economics. Her sister Betty worked for British Airways and her sister Alice worked for the Kenyan consulate in England. They suggested Nancy come to England with the aim of getting an MA before returning to Kenya.

"The fees were £8,000 per year. My only hope of raising that kind of money was to work and save. I took a job as administrator at the Intervention Board part of DEFRA dealing with outbreaks of disease such as Foot and Mouth.

"While living with my sister in Reading, Nanacy was introduced to Jonathan who was to become her husband in 1996.

"When we became a partnership we bought a house in Southmoor near Abingdon. My mother came over for the wedding believing that, as I was marrying an Englishman, I'd never return to Kenya."

"After moving to Oxfordshire I took my first job with the Thames Valley Police Force with the bizarre title of 'Domestic Violence Co-ordinator'. You can imagine the comments that invited, but it allowed me to see how issues interlink and how complex family life can be. My childhood was tough, but when life was difficult there were always adults in the extended family who were there for me. I saw how different it was for children here if their family became dysfunctional after parents split up or one or both became an addict. The children have to cope alone without extended family support. It affects how they see themselves, often not valuing themselves."

Nancy's next job was as an area training officer.

"I loved going out with officers on beat in the city but I found homelessness, often caused by a bad decision or unfortunate event, distressing."

By this time Nancy and Jonathan had two children. Nigel is now 21 and has just finished a degree in business studies after four years studying in Kenya, while Chantelle is fifteen and recently spent one year in school in Kenya.

As well as working full time Nancy had taken a diploma in Management and Leadership at Oxford Brookes after which she took on a new role in the police force. She commuted to Reading to train newly promoted sergeants and inspectors in leadership, management and diversity. Meanwhile in Kenya, in 2000, something happened which would change Nancy's life.

The arrival of an abandoned baby

"My mother was working in a sugar cane field. She heard a baby's cry near the border of her land. This wasn't unusual. Women take their babies with them to work in the fields.

"The next day she heard it again from the same area. On the third day she went to investigate the cries and found a baby of about three months old lying on a blanket with a bundle of clothes next to him. She had arrived just in time. Ants were eating away at his skin. There was no skin left on his heels. She took him to hospital and arranged for him to get treatment.

"When I flew out to visit the family, my mother always came to meet me at the airport. This time she wasn't there and my sister joked 'She has a baby.' When the little boy she found whom she named Moses was not claimed by anyone, she had taken him home and become attached to him. But she was seventy-nine and was struggling to look after the now six-month-old baby.

"With my experience in the British police force, I told my mother off and made her come with me to the police station to sort out the situation. I went to the desk but my mother sat well away looking unhappy. I explained that she was seventy-nine and they should find a home for Moses. My accent gave away the fact that I lived abroad and the officer looked at my Levi jeans and said. 'You have money. You should do it.'

"I found a home for him with Catholic nuns but Moses never forgot my mother. He always recognised her voice when she visited him.

The Nasio Trust is born

"My sister Lorna was poor and eked a living from a kiosk shop at the side of the road. I returned to Kenya in 2003 to discover that Lorna had started feeding orphans and one day, sixty turned up to be fed. With some other women she started the Nasio Women's group. Nasio was the name of my grandmother. It was a hard decision but they chose to support fifteen of the younger orphans by pooling food and organising volunteer teachers."

 But then Lorna suddenly and tragically died of a stroke aged only forty-five. Nancy said:

"Everyone was concerned about what would happen to the orphans. After the funeral I asked to see them. I'll never forget that day. They were distraught; they had lost the person who cared about them. I knew I couldn't walk away. Jonathan and I asked everyone who usually gave us Christmas presents to instead give money to feed the orphans. Before long we had raised over £1,000. We registered the Nasio Trust as a UK charity. To begin with I was the chair of the trustees. Now we have grown so rapidly, we have six trustees and Jonathan is chairman and I direct the charity full time."

 "I hadn't intended dropping my career. Initially I contacted Save the Children and Oxfam and all the big charities I could think of to see if they would take on the project. They work within two hours' drive from the airport and Mumias is eight hours away. I had no choice but to take it on myself."

At it happned Nancy's work in Kenya did have an impact here in Oxfordshire. Nancy explained:

"An officer at Berinsfield was concerned by the lifestyle of some young people there. I suggested showing them a video of the conditions the orphans in Kenya had to cope with including the broken roof of the kiosk kitchen that needed repairing. When we arrived some were drunk and most of them were complaining, effing and blinding about having to watch a boring video. After it finished one of

the girls went into the kitchen came back with some biscuits made them all sit down and said 'What are we going to do to fundraise to repair the roof?'"

The teenagers devised lots of ideas and started to raise the money. "It was much more than we anticipated," continued Nancy. "We were forced by government regulations to demolish the kiosk so we set about raising £30,000 to build a centre. Eventually we raised enough to take four teenagers to Kenya to help paint and decorate it."

The Berinsfield kids were overwhelmed. One young man's father, mother and siblings were all in prison. He told me that he is sure he too would be in prison if I hadn't taken him to Kenya. Suddenly he was valued; the children loved him. He realised he wasn't the bad person he had thought he was and that he could make a different life from the one his background predicted. Now he works and has a child of his own and is a good father."

Since then over 100 young offenders from Berinsfiled, Abingdon and Wantage have been to Kenya to help on Nasio Trust projects and none have reoffended.

From 2005 Nasio took on forty extra orphans each year and needed a bigger centre. Nasio's policy decision is interesting: they do not build orphanages. Nancy explained why:

"Once you put a child in an orphanage away from his community you handicap him. When he leaves he is on his own to readapt into society. Where there is extended family often elderly, the orphan sleeps at home. They come to the support centre in the morning to be fed. If he/she is HIV positive we give them their medication. We provide pre-school education. When they reach primary school age, we buy their uniform (a condition for admission). Our centres are close to the schools so they can have lunch at the centre. We find a family, sometimes staff members, to take on those children with no extended family."

"In 2007 my mother was diagnosed with cancer. I wanted to care for her in the last months of her life. Because I didn't know how long I needed to be away, I chose to resign. Just before she died my mother made me promise that I wouldn't abandon the orphans. 'Whatever you do never leave those children and build a centre in the community where I found Moses.'"

"Hundreds of people came to her funeral we couldn't fit them all in the compound. They had stories to tell of how she had helped them. You don't have to be a hero to change the world. This illiterate old lady had changed the lives of hundreds for the better. When I eventually built the second centre, I named it after her. My uncles said I should have named it after my father. I said 'Why what did he do? He was born to his title but Irene earned the respect of the community.'"

Before returning to England in 2008, I needed time to reflect on what had happened. I decided to climb Kilimanjaro to raise money for Nasio but also to give me the peace and silence to reflect. How could I return to my career with the extra responsibility my mother wanted me to assume? I eventually reached the summit and all the emotions came out. My life had changed forever. I grieved the loss of my mother and the loss of my career but came down in the knowledge that the 140 children Nasio was supporting were my children and I couldn't abandon them."

"If I can only take one thing to Oxtopia it would be Leonardo's Da Vinci's Last Supper. I wasn't exposed to art as a child and it was the first art reproduction I saw. I look at the twelve disciples and realise they had flaws. Whatever our weaknesses we can all change the world for the better we just have to want to."

Nancy Hunt

Born: 1970

Occupation: Director, Nasio Trust

Castaway Items: Leonardo da Vinci's original masterpiece The Last Supper (or a reproduction as in Harris Manchester College)

Original OLE Interview: November 2014

www.thenasiotrust.org

Castaway 3: 16
Roger Neill

Roger Neill can claim to have produced one of the longest running UK TV campaigns – for Fox's Glacier Mints. There is a lot more to the former World President of the International Advertising Association than popular advertising campaigns. He helped Sam Wanamaker realise his life-long dream of rebuilding Shakespeare's Globe.

Roger who lives in King's Sutton near Banbury writes, speaks and conducts master classes and workshops around the world on the subject of creativity and innovation. And having the Orchestra of the Age of Enlightenment as a client means he can persuade their soloists to leave the bright lights and hold concerts in his village church.

Roger's career has made him something of a renaissance man not just here but also in Australia, Asia and the USA. But his life would have been very different if Roger's father had his way. John Neill was a GP in the mining town of Nuneaton in Warwickshire and assumed Roger would follow in his footsteps and study medicine.

Symbol of escape

"I was born on D-Day June 6, 1944 and having 'Graham' as a second name inspired me to make other choices in life. My mother Doris admired her cousin. We all knew him as Bill Browne but the name on his birth certificate was Graham. Early in my life Bill (Graham) Browne became a symbol of escape – a vision of a life beyond the net curtains of Nuneaton. In the Second World War he took part in the landings in Sicily, with the First Dorsets followed by Italy and then the D-Day landings. He was wounded and invalided out from Normandy and awarded the military cross. Given my date of birth, I found that sufficiently inspiring, but Bill was also a champion cyclist and in the 1950s took part in the Monte Carlo Rally.

"I was sent to boarding school, Uppingham in Rutland, where my father insisted I specialise in the sciences. Now I am grateful but at the time my head was in art, literature and music. I didn't want the life my father had mapped out for me so when I sat my 'A' level papers, instead of answering the questions, I wrote letters to the examiners explaining how I wanted to take charge of my life...with the obvious results."

"In 1963, as many of my school mates headed off to university, it looked as if I was unemployable. I went to see Uncle Bill in his Birmingham office to get his advice and see if he would give me a job. Although he didn't offer me work he did give me some advice. He said 'Leave home. Go to London and get a job in a mail room and take it from there.'"

So Roger headed for the capital – it was the height of the 'swinging sixties' and he did find a job as a mail boy with ad agency J Walter Thompson. Roger continued: "It was clear to me that I couldn't afford to live in London on a mail boy's pay so my solution was to take on two extra jobs. I also joined a poker club and played twice a day (lunchtime and evening). Among the members was Llewellyn Thomas, the son of Dylan: he was a fine writer but not a good poker player. My winnings enabled me to live in London."

"I also wrote songs, played the bass guitar and sang in a rock group called The Idle Hands. We played gigs or rehearsed most evenings so my sleeping hours were few. After delivering the mail, in the afternoon, I had a snooze in the mail room. I didn't call it a 'power nap' – it was more about survival and it worked. After a couple of years, I realised that playing poker was a waste of life. I also decided that rock 'n' roll wasn't interesting enough so I switched from rock to classical music.

Consummate ad man

Roger continued: "Although I believed in multiple careers, I resolved to focus in order to achieve something. Concentrating on the day job led me to becoming an account executive for a company that was to become Saatchi and Saatchi. I was lucky enough to be appointed to the board when I was only twenty-seven."

He was being modest attributing his success to luck. Presumably his talent and potential were recognised. The 1970s were early days in TV advertising and incredibly two of Roger's ads are still going strong after four decades.

"Rowntree's who made Fox's Glacier Mints, was my biggest client. I remember that, in the office, our creation – the bear on the glacier – was a pompous chairman of the board and the fox an obnoxious union convenor. "

Roger left Saatchi and Saatchi in 1974 to work for Unilever's advertising agency, Lintas. Roger said,

"I became managing director of the London office which looked after its diverse consumer products interests. Wall's Ice Cream was one of them. I was involved in the successful Wall's Cornetto advert with the operatic jingle which listeners all over the world recall and repeat. After that, the chairman sent me on a tour of Asia with instructions that I should drop in on our Australian office as they hadn't received a visit for a long time."

"In Sydney, we talked ice cream for a bit and then partied for three days before I took the plane home. Back in London, the chairman said 'They seem to like you'. Unknowingly I had undergone an Aussie style interview and passed. I headed back to become Chairman of the Australia/New Zealand branch of Lintas. I spent five blissful years in Sydney. New stuff happened every day and the business seemed to walk in through the door. I was lucky enough to be in the right place at the right time with the outcome that, in 1987, I was asked to return to our London international headquarters as Number Two, a job involving some 100 countries."

In 1990 Roger was elected world president of the trade organisation, the International Advertising Association.

"It was an exciting time, the iron curtain had fallen and I was invited to conferences and to teach in Eastern Europe. Unusually, I was invited to Beijing to chair their first-ever national advertising conference. I faced an audience of 10,000 and had never seen so many delegates at a conference before. The organisers kept asking me for copies of my speech in advance. I never gave it to them because I suspected that it was for censorship purposes. Afterwards some delegates came to speak quietly with me saying, 'We have never heard anything like that before.' I assumed that the translator had translated what I had said accurately because I had talked about how the market economy, democracy, the rule of law and freedom of speech inter-connect with each other."

After twenty-five years in advertising Roger felt that the time had come for a change. His experience with Lintas had given him insight to different kinds of business and their structures and working patterns. He wondered what makes some organisations dynamic, innovative and creative while others fossilise and decline.

"Creative people often think that the manner in which ideas come to fruition in action is serendipity. My work for Rowntree's prior to the launch of Jelly Tots gave me insight that it is not all about luck. I met Vincent Nolan when we trained in the Synectics method at Saatchi and Saatchi (a systematic way of taking new ideas and turning them into action). I joined Synectics as international managing partner helping companies all over the world develop new products and new ways of working."

Restoration man

Roger also continued his multiple career path: "I've organised concerts for thirty years. My first experience was with the last surviving Victorian concert hall in London which was in Blackheath where I lived when I returned from Sydney in 1986. It had been divided up by the council and was run down. A friend came to see me and said 'You're interested in music and know about marketing. We are restoring this great building and need to put on a fund-raising concert, can you help?' It so happened that Prokoviev's son Oleg was living in Blackheath and another resident was Sir Edward Downes, the expert on Russian music, so we imposed on both of them to get involved."

Aussie artists

As well as taking an interest in living artists and musicians Roger also turned his attention to great artists whom we seem to have forgotten. In Australia, he had noticed that many Australians imagine they have no real history apart from aboriginal history.

"They don't pay much attention to the history they have. Because of my love of opera and art I gradually realised they have much to celebrate."

Roger showed me a penetrating portrait of the author Robert Louis Stevenson by Italian-born Count Girolamo Pieri Ballati Nerli who arrived in Australia in November 1885. In August 1892 he visited Apia in Samoa for a month where he met Robert Louis Stevenson. Roger wrote and produced a book about the artist and that portrait.

"Count Nerli's pictures of the author sold so well, he created a production line of them. I set about searching for the original one from 1892. It involved a lot of detective work and my little book is the result."

Roger admires the work of Australian portrait photographer Walter Barnett, who was born in Melbourne in 1862 and curated an exhibition titled Legends: The Art of Walter Barnett for the National Portrait Gallery in Canberra in 2000. It attracted 186,000 visitors. Roger also wrote his entry in the Oxford Dictionary of National Biography in 2006.

"In London Barnett photographed Rodin, the Prince of Wales and Sarah Bernhardt who was the most celebrated actress of her time. Barnett's picture of Sarah Bernhardt is published for the first time in my book. The reason she suppressed it was probably because at sixty-five she preferred to use images of her younger self."

"In London Barnett photographed the famous soprano, Nellie Melba. I've been involved in projects to bring her voice to a new generation. Recorded music was in its infancy when Melba began recording in 1904. She issued over 100 records and helped establish the popularity of the gramophone. After a lot of detective work we found the original metal masters of her records in Germany. That the 78s sound like the sea hitting the shore is due not to quality of the recording but the shellac material of the disc. Through the charity 'Historic Masters' we made new 78s but on vinyl which eliminates that distorting sound and her voice becomes much clearer. I'm working on a project for Decca highlighting the Australian operatic tradition called From Melba to Sutherland featuring seventy-five antipodean singers."

Creativity continued

In 2007, City University in London wanted a director for a new centre for creativity and Roger was interviewed for the post by four professors.

"Before they began to interrogate me, I said 'Do you mind if I ask you a question?' I can't understand why you are interviewing me. The job spec for this post is that applicant should have degrees and I am an ageing rock 'n' roller who worked in the mail room instead of going to university.' They laughed a lot, didn't have much of an answer and gave me the job. We launched a masters in innovation creativity and leadership which has done wonderfully well with many of the students going on to set up their own businesses."

We had talked a lot about Roger's career and artistic interests but not about his family life. "I have two grown up children from my first marriage, Rachel and Kate (one a social worker and the other a teacher of deaf children). I met my second wife, Sophie Wilson, in the early 1990s when I was involved with Sam Wanamaker's project for the re-creation of Shakespeare's Globe in Southwark, London."

"In those days it was just a patch of ground. The chairman of Unilever was also chairman of the Globe and he asked me to help Sam in the role of a part-time unpaid marketing director. It came to fruition with no public funding.

"In my first meeting with Sam I said to him 'I saw you play Iago to Paul Robeson's Othello.' I was thirteen and it was the first time I'd seen a Shakespeare play ▢ it was unforgettable. Sam stopped concentrating on his acting career in order to build the Globe."

Sophie and Roger have a twelve-year-old daughter Dora. For twenty years Sophie has worked as administrator of the Barber Institute of Fine Arts at Birmingham University.

"Living in London was not an option for her and living in Birmingham not an option for me. We took out a map and put a finger down half way between the two and landed on King's Sutton. As a lover of city life, I never imagined living in a village and didn't know whether I would take to it. Now I absolutely adore village life."

What about his castaway object? Roger showed me a picture painted by Oxford artist Helen Duncan.

"This is what I would want to take to the island. We commissioned it for our home and it has lots of personal connections. The Broadwood piano featured was made in 1790 and is used for concerts which we hold regularly in our home. The pianist in the picture is Alissa Firsova who is a brilliant Russian student at the Royal Academy. We have supported her since she was sixteen. The section outside with the lime trees, and Dora floating miraculously above her paddling pool, make this a very personal choice."

Roger Neill

Born: 1944

Occupation: Creative Director for Centre for Creativity, City University London

Castaway Items: Picture painted by Oxford artist Helen Duncan

Original OLE Interview: October 2014

Castaway 3:18
Zoe Broughton

Award-winning video journalist Zoe Broughton has spent more than twenty years campaigning and putting herself on the frontline – going undercover at an animal-testing lab, and dodging landmines while filming secretly in Myanmar. Her zeal for social action has taken her into difficult places where she needs all her courage.

Zoe was born in Louth in Lincolnshire. Her mother, Jenny, was an animal lover and has passed that love on to her daughter. Her father David Broughton was a group captain in the RAF and like most families in the forces they moved often. Zoe's next home was in Buckton, near Huntingdon. Like many children of serving officers Zoe and her brother Sean were sent to boarding school.

"It was an idyllic setting. One boarding house overlooked Ely Cathedral. I like the great outdoors and developed a taste for adventure. The school had a scheme similar to the Duke of Edinburgh's award. I learned how to pitch a tent, to orienteer and to race across rivers balancing on a rope. I loved all that, returning to school coated in mud and taking a shower before heading for breakfast. It was training that has come in useful."

Zoe's 'A' levels were in Biology, English and Economics but her passion for filming and taking photos was well established before she left school. Along with her survival training that passion was to inform her career.

"In 1988, I took a gap year backpacking on my own and headed for Australia where I worked for eight months as an Assistant Sports Instructor in a girls' boarding school. Once I'd earned enough money, I came slowly home via New Zealand and Hawaii."

She went to college to study media studies, computer programming and information technology at the City of London Polytechnic and embarked on an unusual summer job in 1992.

"I began selling juggling equipment for a company called More Balls than Most. I set up stands in Covent Garden and at festivals. I learned to juggle with fire and was asked to take part in a show at a Green Screen event. It was there that I saw Becca Lush and Emma Must speak passionately about their involvement in the Twyford Down road protest."

'The news you don't see on the news'

"I also met two film makers who were making films for NGOs. Thomas Hardy and Jamie Hartzell had become disillusioned with mainstream video journalism and set up Undercurrents. After graduating I joined them along with Paul O'Connor in this first video magazine of direct action. This was long before you could put a film on YouTube. We worked with hi8 (video) tapes, edited on a massive and expensive computer and made about 1,000 VHS copies to distribute. In contrast, nowadays I even make mini films on my iphone and upload them instantly to the web."

"The stated aim of Undercurrents was to make 'the news you don't see on the news'. My first documentary involved spending months filming the M11 protest in East London. At the time I was living in a Quaker-run commune in at the top of Brick Lane in Bethnal Green.

"When the M11 campaigners were evicted from the first houses in the road, I was barricaded into a room with two other women, one of whom had lived in that house for fourteen years. The other was Becca Lush who now works for the charity arm of Lush funding a new generation of social activism. The women put their arms in pipes and encased them in concrete to make it hard to drag them away. After seventeen hours we heard the bailiffs getting closer using a pneumatic drill to get through to us. The women shouted to them to be careful as the room filled with clouds of dust. I kept changing the video tape and hiding it in my socks and knickers. Eventually I was forcibly carried out by police but I was able to keep the camera running.

"On the other side of the road the mainstream press was penned in and not allowed to get near the protestors. Once I was freed I approached the ITN crew, rescued my film from my socks and negotiated the sale of my footage. It appeared that night on the ITN news."

Undercurrents undercover

"Undercurrents was partly funded by Small World. They secured a Channel 4 commission. I was sworn to secrecy when they asked if I would go undercover into Huntingdon Life Sciences, Europe's largest animal testing company to see if the research they had been given, suggesting cruelty and malpractice, could be backed up with evidence.

"The first step was to get a job so I answered an advertisement for a lab assistant in the local paper and got it. For the first two weeks I couldn't film covertly because you have to prove it is in the public interest. I kept a diary of what was going on mostly writing on scraps of paper which I pushed inside my useful socks! On the basis of that we applied to ITC (now OFCOM) for a licence to film. It was granted and I was wired up with a camera built into a pen. The awkward bit was wearing the battery which charged it. At first I was excited but it became emotionally exhausting when I worked with beagle puppies and grew to love them. During stressful test days, puppies were shouted at, shaken and hit. Their squealing was heartrending and the images I filmed still have the power to shock. Damning, from the company point of view, was the unscientific shortcuts taken, fiddling doses, estimating measurements and recording results incorrectly.

"The company was asked to reply to the allegations of animal cruelty. They denounced me, denied my report and sounded confident. It was their word against mine except they didn't realise that I had filmed everything. The edited film was screened on March 29, 1997. The response was amazing. The local police arrested two of the lab technicians. Their licence was revoked until they met conditions demanded by the Home Office. Their share price fell from 126p to 45p."

Zoe's film won The British Environmental Media Award 'Scoop of the Year' and the International Brigitte Bardot Genesis award which she received in Hollywood.

With the fee she was paid for this assignment Zoe was able to buy a houseboat moored off the Donnington Bridge Road and aptly named it Beagle IV.

Zoe's next commission was from Compassion in World Farming. She went to work as an egg packer at a battery hen farm near Oxford.

"I gathered footage of five hens crammed in one cage unable to spread their wings. I filmed a bird stuck on an electric wire put there to keep them from pecking at their eggs as they were conveyed away. My video was sent to all MEPs and as a result they voted in favour of the gradual discontinuation of that method of battery farming. I rescued two hens when I left and put them in an open box in the garden. They had no leg muscles or feathers. It was gripping to watch but they eventually made it out of the box and within five weeks their feathers grew back and they behaved like other hens in a natural environment."

Camera + courage

In other filming for Compassion in World Farming, Zoe's car was stoned by abattoir workers and held at gunpoint by police in Italy. She claims she is not brave but courage is when you feel fear but don't succumb to it. She needed all her courage when she went to film in Myanmar. She went to the refugee camps in Thailand in search of witnesses to an uprising where unarmed students had been mown down by the Burmese military. She said

"I was accompanying a Burmese friend who had survived that protest and obtained refugee status. I had assumed that this would be a safe trip but ended up helping to deliver medical equipment to a camp and being smuggled into

Myanmar across the river in the middle of the night. I experienced first-hand the stress of listening out for the military who could approach at any time."

In 1999, Zoe was given Hostile Regions Training by ex SAS officers. It is a five-day course and is usually very expensive but they give two subsidised places for freelance journalists like Zoe.

"You are taught extreme First Aid, how to film from a window without being in view of a sniper. It trains you in awareness as well as on how to react in dangerous situations. It doesn't protect you completely but I have learnt always to wear a large label saying PRESS."

On a lighter note, Zoe showed me a possible castaway object, a tiny golden charm which came from a great aunt's bracelet. I thought she could smuggle that into Oxtopia in a pocket.

Now that Zoe is a mother of two children, she prefers not to work in violent places. Her partner, Hugh Warwick, is known as 'the hedgehog man' and his best known book *The Prickly Affair* is all about them. Zoe showed me a particularly beautiful imprint of it as a possibility to take on the island. Zoe and Hugh first met at an Undercurrents Christmas party in 1994. They went on a Quaker Course together and made Non Violence for Change looking at non-violence as a strategy. Zoe won more awards and it has been translated into three languages.

"It's a well thought out programme and its section on how to get media coverage is creative and funny.' That was probably useful in her work for Greenpeace since 1997. "Through Greenpeace projects I have secured interviews with people ranging from David Cameron to the Scissor Sisters," she added.

Being a witness

Social activism can raise awareness and change and Zoe's work has helped improve standards of animal welfare but sometimes the results are less dramatic. Zoe believes in being a witness because she says "Injustice hates a witness" and her 'witness' helped save some amazing women from a long prison sentence: The Ploughshares Four including her friend the Nobel Prize nominee Angie Zelter

In January 1996, they slipped past security guards, ran across a frosted runway to the hangar containing Hawk jet number ZH 955 and forced open the door. Then, using household hammers, they smashed the plane's £ 12m sophisticated electronics. Their reason?

"The hawk jet was to be sold to Indonesia and most likely used against the people of East Timor. They were held in custody for six months in Risley Remand Centre before the four went to trial. Before the action took place, I filmed them explaining what they were going to do and which they knew would be called criminal damage but I included in the film scenes of the massacre in East Timor."

In Zoe's film were planted the seeds of their defence that their action was intended to stop the greater crime of genocide. John Pilger appeared as a witness and when the 'confession' film was shown in court, the jury were visibly moved by the scenes they witnessed and they found the four women 'Not Guilty'.

Zoe bought a house in East Oxford and she and Hugh married in the Friends Meeting House in 2003, the year after she filmed in Myanmar. Their first child was Matilda and she was delivered at home by Kirsten Baker, partner of fellow castaway Jeremy Spafford. In 2006 their son Tristan Pip was born. Zoe is rarely far from a camera but she prefers being behind it rather than in front. But Hugh had other ideas and filmed the birth of Matilda and since then Kirsten has used that film to train other midwives. Parenthood has not slowed Zoe down and in her spare time she loves to play the hectic sport of 'Ultimate Frisbee'.

In 2013, two of Zoe's friends in Greenpeace were arrested in the Arctic trying to spread the word about danger to the Arctic from Russian oil exploration. Philip Ball and Frank Hewetson were among thirty activists held in a Russian prison with a threat of a fifteen-year sentence hanging over them.

"I filmed them before they left for the protest. Phil told his family he could be away for three weeks. I went on a vigil for them in Headington and met Phil's mum. I was able to film them once they were together again. At that vigil I met the folk singer Peggy Seeger [Castaway 2: 8] and have since made several musical videos with her."

For her castaway object Peggy didn't want to make a big footprint. She took her favourite pebble which she thought could disappear into the beach. But she added, "I can't go without my camera, and its memory card will have pictures of family, friends and of Oxford. Pip is a chorister at Magdalen College School and it is a beautiful experience watching the choir sing in such a beautiful setting. After moving out of the narrow boat into a house, I didn't lose my love of rivers. I share ownership of a canoe and that would be great on the island."

As her camera is often around her neck, I thought we could allow her to take her canoe as well. Perhaps she will use it to travel back to Oxford where she shares her skills as a tutor at Film Oxford teaching how to make low budget films and films on smart phones.

Zoe Broughton

Born: 1970

Occupation: Video film maker and campaigner

Castaway Items: Golden charm from a great aunt's bracelet; *A Prickly Affair* by Hugh Warwick; a camera, and canoe

Original OLE Interview: January 2016

Castaway 3:19

Qu Leilei

A founder of the first Chinese contemporary art movement – The Stars (1979), Qu Leilei has had such an extraordinary life in a volatile time in China's history. He has done many things in his sixty-four years, and like the cat has had nine distinct lives; but there is one thread which runs through it, his passion to draw and paint.

My first encounter with Leilei was at the preview of his exhibition at the Ashmolean Museum in 2005. Everyone's Life is an Epic consisted of twenty-one striking contemporary portraits. Each subject had been asked by the artist to describe their philosophy of life. Under his portrait the homeless man had written 'You are not a failure until you give up trying' and his chiseled features were surrounded by bold colour with the Chinese translation in calligraphy that was integral to the work. East and West had met in this brush. I returned several times to this exhibition and was commissioned to write a profile feature on the artist. I soon learned that the epic life was Leilei's.

What a life journey from when he arrived here in 1985 owning just $35 and a roll of paintings. He earned his living how he could while he improved his English. He worked as a pavement artist in Piccadilly Circus, washed dishes in Chinese restaurants, cleaned houses and typed features in Mandarin. Why did such a talented artist need to do that and will he take art from East or West onto our mythical island of Oxtopia?

Life one: childhood

"When I was born in the province of Heilongjiang in Manchuria, my parents Qu Bo and Lu Bo expected that my brother Jingjing and sister Miaomiao and I would grow up there. I was only four when the unexpected happened and we were uprooted and too young to realise how unusual were my parents. By this time, my mother was managing a large hospital and my father, although only twenty-eight, was a senior party official in charge of a work force of over 20,000 people. His factory manufactured railway rolling stock and was the biggest employer in the city of Qiqihar (northwest of Harbin)."

"As a small child you take your circumstances for granted but I was aware of how people treated him as their local hero. There was no jealousy among the workers who circulated stories of his valour fighting in the civil war. His limp was testimony to his battle injuries but his handsome face was unscarred so he looked the part, too."

"Railways were glamorous in those days but unlike his work force, some local politicians were jealous of his meteoric rise. For a party with ideals of socialism, the local Communist Party was a hot bed of factionalism and personal ambition. Our lives were cast under a dark shadow when my father's enemies suspended him and he had to submit to a period of self-criticism. In the Chinese Communist Party that is not a private matter: self-criticism is a public performance intended as humiliation. Young and energetic and suddenly faced with a life confined to home, he turned to writing as a positive outlet for his frustration. Through it, he relived his experiences fighting the bandits allied to Chiang Kai-shek's forces, in the mountains of Manchuria. He called his novel *Tracks in the Snowy Forest* and that could be a reminder of my father to take to Oxtopia."

Later Madame Mao used it for one of her model operas. Qu Bo's career was to blossom again when he was transferred to Beijing. They even enjoyed a grace and favour home within the grounds of the exquisite Summer Palace.

"At school I had little choice for portraits and I painted the same subjects over and over again. Any subjects apart from Chairman Mao and revolutionary heroes were frowned upon. Everywhere you looked in school, on the street, and at home, there were pictures of him. His features were etched into my soul. Another subject was our leader's favourite, some say invented but certainly conveniently dead, revolutionary hero, Lei Feng. He was a model ordinary soldier who came from a poor family. Lei Feng's ambition was to become a cog in the revolutionary machine and Mao liked that so much that he wanted every Chinese to copy him! As a child, I sketched our idol climbing mountains of knives and plunging deep into a sea of flames all for Chairman Mao."

One of Qu Leilei's latest paintings on display in the British Museum is called *Lei Feng*. Only this time there is a satirical edge to the portrayal. *Lei Feng* is depicted as a terracotta warrior, all sense of self obliterated.

Having succeeded in getting the young people of China to hero worship him, Mao was able to turn these radicalised youth against their parents' generation in the Cultural Revolution which began in 1966. Leilei's father was humiliated, his mother sent to labour camp, his brother to prison and Leilei was beaten up and interrogated.

Life two: midshipman

His father found a way of getting Leilei enlisted in the navy on the island of Hainan. He remained safe until his 'undesirable background' was discovered and he was discharged and sent back to Beijing. End of that story!

Life three: peasant

Salvation came when, in 1968, like all educated youth, Leilei was sent into the countryside to be re-educated as a peasant. Leilei explained:

"In Wimbledon where I now live, it rarely snows and the winters are often warm, wet and grey. After my daughter Taotao was born in 1996, I took a walk in the park.

All around me was transformed. I had never seen it like this before. I stopped to sketch the scene. It was innocent, even virginal. The crisp white snow did not last long but for a while the world around me shone as brightly as my heart radiated love. As I sketched, I remembered a time when I did not possess the paper to draw the beauty around me. Each of my nine lives has exposed me to a different landscape. Remembering my life as a peasant, I have a vision of a dark purple sky that reflected blue on the frozen snow of Manchuria."

Life four: barefoot doctor

While he still had to work in the fields, Leilei was given the opportunity to embark on another life as a barefoot doctor.

"My qualification for the role was non-existent. I was simply provided with a copy of *A Barefoot Doctor's Manual* (possibly useful in Oxtopia!) The name arose because we were meant to live like the peasants we served and they preserved their precious shoes whenever possible for use when they weren't working in the fields. Armed with this medical bible, I was to care for people in this vast semi wilderness where there were no doctors. It was terrifying and yet flattering that grown men and women came to me for help and advice, trusted and confided in me. Armed with my manual and a clinic stocked with basics like penicillin, antibiotics, acupuncture needles, surgical spirit, aspirin, paracetamol and a sterilizer I tried to live up to my patients expectations."

Leilei enjoyed his eighteen months as a barefoot doctor. Meanwhile in Beijing life was improving and Qu Bo found a new career for Leilei but he was a reluctant recruit into his fifth life.

Life five: soldier

"I was expected to enlist in The People's Liberation Army. Although angry and disappointed I said nothing. I tried not to show my feelings because I saw that my mother and father were happy. Everyone expected that I should be delighted with this arrangement which was the pinnacle of desirability in Cultural Revolutionary China."

Qu Leilei described one of the most bizarre assignments: "My pai (platoon) was one of the propaganda teams sent to fight the revolutionary fight against the academic establishment. We were posted to the National Academy of Science. Our task was to re-educate the best brains in China! We were mostly nineteen-year-olds and some of my fellow soldiers couldn't even write their names properly! My pai was assigned to the Department of Metallurgy and our guinea pigs were the thirty to forty scientists plus lab assistants. While there we joined an audience of 2,000 to watch a film. The head of the propaganda team stood up and addressed everyone, 'This film will show you what the Americans are doing. We must criticise this. Don't be taken in by them. This project is just designed to make money to further the capitalist ideal.'

What was this movie? I was riveted to my seat, as the film started to roll and showed Apollo orbiting the moon. I could not believe what was before my eyes when I watched Neil Armstrong walking on the moon. I thought this must be 'make believe'. But I sensed the mood of the scientists was one of excitement. We were watching a dream become reality but this incredible achievement was not even reported in China. Only, the scientific community was allowed to know these things. Only the scientists and a few platoons of soldiers who happened to be occupying the Academy at the time – and some of them fell asleep!"

When the Cultural Revolution drew to a close Leilei was able to leave the army.

Life six: a lighting technician at China TV

Leilei had rediscovered his love of art by sketching in the margins of military magazines. Now he recalled how, in 1976, he was sent by China TV to TangShang which had just been devastated by an earthquake.

"We were the lucky ones supplied with tents and clean water. In the evening we could do nothing but survey the panorama of a city in ruins. Tangshan was flattened like Hiroshima after the Bomb. I took out my sketchbook and began to draw obsessively. My sketches were completely spontaneous. They flowed like water from my fingers. The results were unlike anything I had done before. A dam in my brain had burst and new images appeared on the paper. A face with a single tear drop becoming a river...an eye in the wind, soldiers drawn not as humans but machine men on wheels crushing flowers and everything of beauty beneath them, a heavy figure but with hair blown lightly in the wind. Page after page, I drew."

Life seven: the artist

In 1976, Mao died and Deng Xiaoping gradually took hold of the reins of power and created the China we see today. He allowed the creation of a Democracy Wall at Zidan (in 1978). This was to be a beacon of hope for two years. Young poets, artists and those who wanted to think the unthinkable came to together to create new magazines. Leilei met other artists who were inspired by western art and a desire for self-expression. They called themselves The Stars☐. The other four leaders were Huang Rui, Wang Keping, Ma Desheng and Yang Li. They tried to find a gallery to display their work without success. They decided to hold an 'illegal' exhibition hanging their work on the railings outside the National Gallery. (Among the twenty artists displaying work was Ai Weiwei.)

People flocked to see this new art and reacted positively. When the police closed the exhibition, two political activists, Lui Qing and Xu Wenli encouraged them to march to Tiananmen Square. Leilei described that momentous day.

"While Ma [Desheng] addressed the crowd, Wang Keping and I held it up a banner reading 'In politics we want democracy and in art we want freedom.' As we marched I carried a placard which I am not sure how many understood! It said 'Kollwitz is our flag and Picasso our pioneer'. Word had got around and more than two thousand people joined us as we marched towards the Central Government building. As we drew near, we saw that we were expected. Hundreds of white uniformed police had blocked the road ahead. The tension facing this

wall of white was so intense that you could almost touch it. Then someone burst into 'The Internationale'. We all joined in and the sound inspired me and helped overcome my fear. I had no doubts; I believed in the rightness of our protest even more passionately as we approached the solid unmoving ranks of police. I felt the huge responsibility and dignity of this march."

"Suddenly the singing stopped and I turned to look. The people behind melted away into the sides of the street. Only twenty of us were left facing the police cordon. We could not run. We were the leaders. Each of us remained calm even though our hearts were racing. The police said 'Our orders are to stop you going on to Tiananmen.' They were expecting a fight but Liu Qing and Xu Wenli said 'We will follow police instructions and change our route.' We avoided confrontation by turning right and heading in the direction of the Beijing local government building. Wang Keping and I climbed its steps and held the banner aloft. Huang Rui made a speech and Liu Qing and Xu Wenli went inside. They found just three people in this huge building. Everyone else was on holiday! The international press arrived on the scene and took our pictures and we hurried home before the police could arrest us."

The Stars went on to have an exhibition inside the National Gallery and to be celebrated but a day was near that would catapult Leilei into his next life as an exile.

"My friend Wei Jingsheng [the most famous of the early democracy campaigners] had been arrested on March 29, 1979 after publishing an article warning people to make sure 'Deng Xiaoping does not generate into a dictator.' He pasted it on the Democracy Wall calling for a 'genuine general election'.

"It was really all down to chance. The assignment for lighting technicians was in rotation. My name just happened to be on the rota for the following day's filming at the High Court. I would be present at my friend's trial. I felt so tired and concerned for him that I went to bed early. Just before midnight I was woken by the doorbell. On the doorstep were Liu Qing, Xu Wenli and two others. Liu said 'We have been able to get this tiny tape recorder.' For 1979 it was advanced technology supplied by Li Shuang's [another artist-activist] future husband, a diplomat in the French Embassy but that is another story. 'Is it possible for you to record the trial tomorrow? It will be a show trial but Wei will act as his own defence and we would like to know what he says.' It was a heavy responsibility they were asking of me. I did not feel fear although perhaps I should have been afraid."

Leilei recorded the trial and Liu Qing and Xu Wenli pasted the transcript on the Democracy Wall where it was seen by the international press. Wei Jingsheng believes that saved his life. But it led to the destruction of the Democracy Wall and the imprisonment of Liu Qing and Xu Wenli. From then on Qu Leilei's life became increasingly unbearable and which he described as being kept in 'small shoes'. In 1985 he was able to leave China and arrived here as an exile to face new challenges.

Life eight: the exile

"I delighted in the freedom from political pressure but discussed the situation with my younger sister CuiCui who was already here as a student. 'How can I earn my living? I am thirty four and yet I must start over again from zero.'" And from zero, he struggled until he got his first exhibition organised by the war correspondent Edith Lederer in her home. In 1986 the Holland Gallery mounted a show called East and West and invited Leilei to take part. This was followed by joint exhibitions in the Royal Festival Hall and the Pompidou Centre and solo shows in the Tricycle and Redfern galleries. His career in the UK was taking off.

Life nine: Family man and teacher

In 1989, an artist called Caroline Dean sought his advice. She was on course to go to Beijing for a year when the events of Tiananmen Square happened. Should she go? That too is a long story but one with a happy ending. They married and built a good life together and their daughter Taotao was born in 1997. Caroline introduced Leilei to adult and continuing education including at the Ashmolean. He became a successful teacher publishing many 'How To' books for arts and crafts publisher Cico Books.

But he still dreamed of being a full time artist and eventually that dream came true. His work is recognised around the world including in the country of his birth. In 2011 he was given a one man show in the National Gallery Beijing and a biopic of him on China TV. In the UK, he is honorary president of the Chinese Brush Painters Society.

After his nine lives what will he want to inspire his tenth life on Oxtopia ?

"I have admired Rembrandt's portraits since my first sight of prints of them but I don't think I could be happy on the island without a supply of artist's tools and materials so that I could paint my fellow Oxtopians. Life on Oxtopia will suit me because Caroline and I hope to retreat to the wilds of Devon to concentrate on painting and maybe do a bit of Tai Chi.

Qu Leilei

Born: 1951

Occupation: Artist

Castaway Items: Artist's tools and materials; Qu Bo's *Tracks in the Snowy Forest*

Original OLE Interview: February 2016

www.quleilei.net

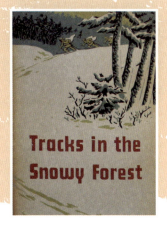

Tracks in the Snowy Forest

Castaway 3:20

Francesca Kay

At the beginning of April authors from around the world descend on Oxford for our world famous Literary Festival, but one author who won't have far to travel to promote her latest book is Francesca Kay. Although this award-winning novelist put down roots in Oxford two decades ago, she's led a nomadic life.

Born in Kensington, Francesca moved with her parents to Hong Kong when she was a baby. She spent much of her early childhood in Southeast Asia. Her father Bernard was English and her mother Teresa is of Indian origin, from Mumbai. Teresa comes from a Catholic family whose culture was always more British than Indian. Indeed Bernard and Teresa met as students at Oxford in 1947. Unlike her fellow students, Teresa was excited by that legendary cold winter, as it provided her first experience of snow.

Francesca and her family returned to London briefly, in time for her to start school. One of her abiding memories of her short time at the Virgo Fidelis Junior School in the Old Brompton Road is being taught to curtsy deeply to the nuns.

"I was the last child in my class to learn to read but the first to finish the set of Janet and John books. It doesn't matter if you start late; what counts is enthusiasm as a reader later on."

Considering that self-confessed slow learner has become an award winning writer, her comments are encouraging for all those parents who are concerned about the speed, or lack of it, of their child's progress.

Francesca's father was a diplomat, and during her childhood his Foreign Office postings included Hong Kong, Singapore and the Philippines. It was in Hong Kong that her two sisters, Benedicta and Cordelia, were born. The family left Hong Kong when Francesca was five years old but she has vivid memories of it, especially of playing with a pet gibbon called Jacko.

"Every year or two we moved to a new country", said Francesca. "Moving so frequently from place to place had drawbacks; we were rather rootless children, and leaving behind the amahs and ayahs who cared for us was always very sad. But later on, that nomadic childhood turned out to be quite useful to a writer. Travel can make one more observant, more understanding of difference."

She learned to adapt to new schools with new systems and to make new friends.

"It was rather bizarre that in the heat of the Philippines our school uniform consisted of Stuart tartan skirts.''

Francesca explained that her vision of home was not England but India and one particular place.

"For holidays we headed for Mumbai and the seaside suburb of Bandra. That was where my grandparents lived. When I was a little girl, their house overlooked the sea, and from my bedroom window at night I would watch the reassuring flash of the distant lighthouse. But now that land has been reclaimed and built on and the sea view has become a view of a luxury hotel."

She got to know other parts of India too. An uncle lived first in Shimla and then in Kashmir, where she and her family had wonderful lakeside and mountain holidays. When her father was posted to Delhi, she felt completely at home. But from there he was sent to Laos and the contrast was great. At that time Laos was next door to a war zone and life was quite restricted. Instead of going to school, Francesca was taught by her mother (who had read English at Oxford) at home.

A bookish education

In 1969, aged eleven, Francesca found herself alone on a plane heading for England and for Woldingham, a Catholic boarding school in Surrey.

"I arrived at Woldingham in the summer term. The nuns thought it would be easier for me starting the year then because the weather would be warm. But that meant I was the only new child in the school. Being rather foreign, and definitely a bit precocious as the result of my bookish education, I was an object of curiosity for a while."

"But I soon learned to fit in. I loved the surrounding countryside, the bluebell woods and the light summer evenings. On the whole I have happy memories of school and many of my friends from that time are still friends to this day. As we grew up together at close quarters, we are quite like siblings."

"I always loved writing. I had note books filled with poems. When I was eleven the poems rhymed but by the time I was in my teens, I had ambitions to be rather more modernist and sophisticated. I had an amazing English teacher – Angela Watkins – a huge influence on me. She looked a bit scatty because she was always in a hurry, rushing in to the classroom at the last minute, her arms full of mimeographed sheets she had just rolled off. I can still recall the smell of the purple ink on paper hot off the press – the scent of literature to me. Of course she taught her classes the set books, but she was determined that all of us should read more widely. She used to begin each lesson with a new poem or a piece of prose which we discussed together. That experience probably helped when I applied to read English at Somerville."

"I loved my time at Oxford, and among my inspirational tutors were the poet Bernard O'Donoghue and the Shakespearean scholar, Professor Katherine Duncan-Jones. After graduating, I had visions of moving to Italy and making films but instead, rather haphazardly, I took the exam for the fast stream of the Civil Service and I passed."

Francesca's Civil Service career was short-lived but significant because it was then that she met her husband, Mark. Her early married life replicated her childhood in some respects as she accompanied him on his postings to Jamaica, the US and Germany.

"I recognised the furnishings. Wherever we went, the bedspreads and the lamp shades were the same as the ones we'd had when I was a child. But I enjoyed the travelling life because I enjoy discovering new places".

Francesca feels that in many ways she was lucky. Although her career was shortcut, it allowed her to spend time with her children, Susannah, Arabella and Joseph, a luxury that many women do not have. In 1996 the family settled in Oxford.

Oxford and writing roots

"We have put down roots and this is 'home'. I am sometimes seized by wanderlust but Oxford is one of the most beautiful cities in the world and it has great people in it, so I plan to stay."

We began to talk about her writing and its origins.

"I have always enjoyed telling stories. I used to make my younger sisters sit still and listen while I told them interminable tales. And I told my children stories too. Once the children were settled in their schools, I had the silence and the space to start trying to write seriously. I could never have done it with the noise of lively children in the background."

The central character of Francesca's first book, *An Equal Stillness*, is a painter.

"I studied art history at 'A' level and art remains very important to me. When I was writing *An Equal Stillness*, I looked in particular at the art of the early twentieth century and abstract art, *Black Square* (1913) by the Russian painter Kasimir Malevich, for instance. It caused me to think about ways of eliminating unnecessary detail in life and focusing on what is central."

The Malevich is a possible castaway work of art, together with Ben Nicholson's 1935 *White Relief* or Barbara Hepworth's 1932 *Two Heads*. Francesca said, "I think Barbara Hepworth is a very great artist. She was the inspiration for *An Equal Stillness*, a novel which celebrates the creative life but also counts its costs."

Writing a book in today's competitive publishing environment is only the beginning. It is followed by the struggle to find a publisher but find one she did. Weidenfeld and Nicolson took her on and in 2009 *An Equal Stillness* won the Orange Award for New Writers (a prize which sadly no longer exists).

"It was open to any woman writing in English from anywhere in the world. Winning it gave me a real confidence boost. I felt I could dare to call myself a 'writer' without being delusional."

A slightly more confident Francesca sat down to write her second novel, *The Translation of Bones*, which is about the lives, dreams and memories of a London congregation united only by their place of worship. The fine line between illusion and reality is something that fascinates her.

Ruth Gledhill in *The Times* said, "Francesca Kay's power lies in the shock of deliberate understatement." That power led to *The Translation of Bones* being longlisted for the Orange Prize, and now she has given us her third novel, *The Long Room*.

"On one level it's a spy novel but it is also a book about loneliness, about what can happen when a young man with a head full of poetry is starved of human contact and desperate for love.".

We had arrived at the point where I needed to pin down Francesca's island choice. She had talked of Malevich and Barbara Hepworth. So would her final choice be a work of art?

"If I could only have one image to contemplate for the rest of my life, it would be Piero della Francesca's *Resurrection* (1460s). But that should be seen in a sacred space, not a personal one and, like all great art, should be accessible to everyone, not hidden away in private. So instead I'll take a birthday card my children made for me years ago, when they were young".

It is special as it includes charming childish self-portraits and drawings of things that are important to Francesca, so unsurprisingly she has framed it. Then she remembered that she would want to continue writing on Oxtopia (she used a fountain pen to write her novel).

"Writing is like any discipline," she said, "the more you practice, the better you get – I hope!"

Francesca Kay

Occupation: Author

Castaway Items: A framed birthday card from her children

Original OLE Interview: May 2016

The Long Room is published by Faber and Faber.

Andrew McMichael

When he's not searching for a vaccine against Aids, the Oxford University Professor of Molecular Medicine Sir Andrew McMichael likes skiing, walking and climbing mountains. His route to the summit of science has been an exciting but long climb requiring patience and determination which led him to become part of the world famous Oxford Clinical School.

"In 1983, Sir David Weatherall approached the Medical Research Council (MRC) with the suggestion that a small institute could be developed in the Oxford Clinical School to apply the techniques of molecular and cell biology to study human disease. From those small beginnings with a few researchers, which fortunately included me, it has become extraordinarily successful. It now employs over 450 clinical and non-clinical scientific, technical and support staff from all over the world. The visiting scientists and students come from more than twenty four countries."

In the last thirty-five years, the Oxford Clinical School has risen to become number 1 or 2 in the world and Professor McMichael has been part of that extraordinary story.

"Recent advances in molecular and cell biology have enormous potential for medical research and practice. Initially they were most successfully exploited for determining the causes of genetic diseases and how to control them. Gene technology is revolutionising all aspects of medical research, advancing understanding of disease, diagnostics, treatments and approaches to vaccines."

"It has spawned a biotechnology industry and should help us gain insights into broader aspects of human biology, including development, ageing and evolution."

From his sitting room in Beckley he pointed beyond his low garden wall to fields looking out towards Otmoor being grazed by some unusual cattle with a broad white stripe around their middle.

"Our neighbours and Kate (his wife) and I bought those twenty acres to save them from the threat of development. I was pleasantly surprised when the farmer who rents them from us brought Belted Galloway cattle into the fields. Galloway in South West Scotland is where my family originated and my father's cousin used to breed Belted Galloways. Nearly all my childhood holidays were spent there."

Medicine in the genes

Andrew may have a Scottish name but he grew up in Richmond and went to St Pauls School. At home medicine was in his genes.

"My father Sir John McMichael was a renowned cardiologist and met my mother, Sybil, when he was working at Hammersmith Hospital. She was working as a radiographer at the time."

His father was Director of the Royal Postgraduate Medical School and pioneered research into the causes of heart failure and developed diagnostic methods which underlie many modern treatments of heart disease.

"From an early age medical research was part of our everyday conversation and my brothers and I met his medical friends when they came to dinner. We visited the hospital a lot, including Christmas morning when my father would go to the cardiac ward to carve the turkey."

Oxford is a small city and I often discover connections between the castaways I am privileged to interview. In Sir Andrew's case the connection was with Sir Roger Bannister. Their first encounter was at one of those dinner parties at home when Sir Roger was a young senior house physician working for his father, just after his four-minute mile. Later on the two families connected here in Oxford.

"My younger brother Peter became an engineer so it wasn't a given that I would follow in my father's footsteps. But, when I decided to go into medicine, I determined not to follow him into cardiology – too large an act to follow."

In 1962, Andrew headed for Cambridge to Gonville and Caius College to read medicine. "At that time the gender balance was about 9 :1 male: female. It made for a pressure cooker environment concentrating on work. I made good friends there but girl friends had to come from London."

When home in London in the vacation a school friend introduced him to Kate. "Kate and my relationship developed quickly when we shared our passion for walking and climbing. Kate said, "Our first date was at Harrison's Rocks, a rocky outcrop near Tunbridge Wells. I knew that if I didn't get up the climb I didn't stand a chance. I did!"

After Cambridge, he went to St Mary's Paddington to do his three years clinical training. Andrew, as a young house doctor worked long hours and moved every six months for three years while getting experience in different fields of medicine, including a short locum house job in neurology with Roger Bannister at St Mary's Paddington." During these three years "I worked one night on and one night off and one weekend in two."

He married Kate in 1968 and she said "He was known for falling asleep at dinner parties after a night 'on'!" Fortunately for him, Kate also had a demanding job teaching in Tower Hamlets. She said: "If you watched 'Call the Midwife' you'll have an accurate picture of the area as it was then. It was such hard work with sole responsibility for forty children."

Into immunology

"When I passed my membership exams for the Royal College of Physicians, it felt like a gateway to a life-long career had opened. But it was a chance event which led me into immunology. Kate was pregnant with Fiona and was attending the anti-natal clinic at St Mary's. When I went to pick her up, I bumped into the distinguished scientist and Professor of Medicine there, Sir Stanley Peart. He asked if I was looking for a job and wondered if I was interested in research."

"I said I was but didn't want to follow my father into cardiology: I was interested in the immune system, one of the few areas my father knew little about! He offered to introduce me to a colleague at the National Institute for Medical Research in Mill Hill and recommended that I put my clinical training on hold and concentrate on research full time."

That colleague was Ita Askonas, a distinguished Canadian scientist, and she became Andrew's PhD supervisor along with Alan Williamson.

"In 1974, I obtained a PhD in Immunology at Mill Hill. Ita and I became very good friends and remained so until she died last year aged eight-nine. She helped a lot throughout my career.

"At that time, we knew about basic antibodies and simple vaccinations but ninety per cent of what we now know about the immune system we have learned since 1974. Then, we were just learning that T cells, which develop in the thymus, a lymphoid gland in the chest, are responsible for graft rejection. Now we know that they control virus infections and most types of immunity."

"After Mill Hill, I wanted to connect my research to something clinical. Professor Hugh McDevitt in California was working with Oxford geneticist Walter Bodmer. They were interested in tissue types and especially something called HLA.

"If you have the wrong HLA tissue type you will reject organ grafts. Almost everyone not closely related has inherited different HLA types so this has been a big problem in transplantation. HLA types are highly variable and complex. In 1973 it had been discovered that some diseases, such as one type of arthritis, were more common in people with particular HLA types. I decided that was the area I wanted to research.

California dreaming

"The obvious thing to do was head for California to work with Hugh. There, we had the time of our lives. I worked in a stellar scientific environment and enjoyed spending weekends with Kate and our two older children outside in the perfect climate, camping in places like Yosemite Valley. In 1976 I was offered a permanent job at Stanford and it was tempting. But we had family in the UK and we felt this is where our roots were we would be more connected with the rest of the world in the UK compared to California in those pre-internet days."

Deciding to come back home involved a big risk: the post in California was permanent, well paid with good prospects and they returned to the UK in 1977 with only one year employment guaranteed with a grant from the Welcome Trust to work in Oxford.

"My first grant was used to look at the role of T cell immunity in influenza virus infection working once again with Ita. I am lucky that things worked out well. In 1977, the Nuffield Department of Clinical Medicine had four or five senior scientists and now it must have 300. The expansion has been huge. The Oxford Medical School began in a wing of the Old Radcliffe Infirmary and moved to the John Radcliffe in 1979, and in 1989 the Weatherall Institute was built on the JR site. When John Bell became Regius Professor, he wanted to build a new Institute of Medical Genetics on one of the car parks. As that wasn't possible he turned his eye towards the green fields at the Churchill. The result is there for all to see. Andrew now works in one of the new institutes on that site.

"I found myself working with extraordinary people like David Weatherall, Peter Morris (Professor of Surgery) and later John Bell (Regius Professor), so the gamble of returning paid off. I have been fortunate to be part of the extraordinary growth of clinical research in Oxford."

Designing the HIV vaccine

Andrew showed me a beautiful picture which he explained was of an HLA molecule.

"Some American scientists Pamela Bjorkman, Jack Strominger and Don Wiley were able to make this image of the crystal structure of an HLA molecule. This is the top end view and is magnified over a million times."

He pointed to a small area of pink.

"These are the peptide fragments of cellular proteins, which would include virus peptides if the cell was infected. From my perspective, this is the most influential paper in immunology of the last fifty years."

"Following this paper the study of human immunology took off across the globe. I was by then focusing on HIV, looking at why some people do better than others. One thing shown by the HLA crystal is that all the genetic variability in HLA occurs around the groove that binds the peptides. Therefore different people respond to a virus, such as HIV, in different ways and people with certain HLA types have better resistance to HIV." Andrew continued, "This information is central to our design of the HIV vaccine we are developing in Oxford."

Much of his vaccine development programme is funded by the Centre for HIV Vaccine Immunology – the CHAVI programme – which is based in Duke University in North Carolina and funded by a grant from the US National Institutes for Health.

"This is a very intensive collaborative programme and I have international telephone conferences two or three times a week and visit the US six times a year, working with exciting groups of scientists with different areas of expertise."

"Science is a global activity, all conducted in the English language, and Oxford is well connected internationally. Besides our overseas collaborations, we have scientists who come here from all over the world. I love that aspect of my work."

In addition to his HIV work, Andrew also keeps up an interest in influenza. Given the constant threat of a new influenza virus pandemic, he is also working with the MRC and the Wellcome Trust on the flu-watch programme, monitoring influenza virus infection in 2,000 healthy volunteers. The study is designed to determine whether pre-existing T cell immunity protects against natural influenza virus infection.

"Because of the threat of Avian flu we have also developed very strong links with Beijing and there are senior Chinese scientists working here with us on the immunology and cell biology of influenza. These collaborations with China are particularly exciting."

Love of mountains

Away from the lab, Professor McMichael (he was knighted in 2006) maintains his love of the great outdoors.

"Although we don't do serious climbing now, we bought an old farmhouse in La Salle les Alpes in France seven years ago. We ski in the winter and walk in the summer. The visitors' book from the house with its photographs of family, including six grandchildren, and friends would be a nostalgic memento for a desert island."

Andrew showed me some of his mountaineering books including an old edition of Scrambles in the Alps by Edward Whymper, the first man to climb the Matterhorn.

"Once on the top, and before the tragedy on the descent, Whymper looked at the wonderful view from the summit towards the south west and the mountains near our French house (the Pelvoux, Ecrins and Meije) which he described as his first love. He opened up the sport of mountaineering in that area and they have even built a statue of him near the village – it's unusual to find a statue of an Englishman in France.

Andrew showed me his favourite mountaineering book Mountains: An Anthology by Antony Kenny who was pro-vice chancellor of the University of Oxford from 1984 to 2001.

So what would be his final choices for Oxtopia?

"If I took this watercolour by our daughter Fiona it would remind me of our growing family. Fiona lives in Surrey with her husband Robbie and has three children. She trained as an architect but has recently started her own business, Fiona Lauchlan Art."

Andrew also plumped for the Nature paper by Pam Bjorkman and colleagues, containing the groundbreaking crystal images.

"Science is often thought to be esoteric and inaccessible, but this paper and the image shows that science can be beautiful. This crystal profoundly influenced all my scientific thinking over the last twenty-seven years".

Sir Andrew McMichael

Born: 1943

Occupation: Professor of Molecular Medicine

Castaway Items: Watercolour by his daughter Fiona; Nature paper by Pam Bjorkman and colleagues, containing groundbreaking crystal images

Original OLE Interview: June 2014

Castaway 3:22

Pauline Goddard

Pauline Goddard is the Chairman of the Oxfordshire Federation of Women's Institutes and in 2015 the WI celebrated its centenary. I assumed the WI was quintessentially English but I was wrong: it was a Canadian invention. The idea crossed the Atlantic and the first British branch was formed in Wales in 1915 in Llanfair pwllgwyngyllgigerychwyrndrobwllllantysiliogogogoch: really.

From its foundation in 1915, the WI became a tool to revitalise rural communities and to encourage women to become more involved in producing food during the First World War. That is where the association of the WI with jam as a means of preserving food began. At the outbreak of the Second World War, the general secretary of the WI ordered 430 tons of sugar to distribute for jam making. And as for baking, the WI have been doing it for a hundred years – long before the idea of *The Great British Bake Off* was a twinkle in the BBC's eye.

Today the WI's aims have broadened and it has become the largest voluntary women's organisation in the UK. Nationally it has over 6,600 branches and 142 of them are in Oxfordshire. The WI headquarters is in London but as Pauline Goddard observes, "Oxfordshire is lucky because Denman College, the WI National Education Centre, is right on our door step in Marcham just outside Abingdon."

Denman College used to be called Marcham Park and was used by the RAF during the Second World War. After the war the WI bought it and turned it into a college. It was launched in 1948 and was named after Lady Denman who was the national chairman for thirty-three years. A new teaching block was opened by the Queen Mother in 1970 and the Home Economics Centre was opened by Queen Elizabeth II in 1977.

A High Wycombe life

Pauline's background was somewhat more modest than that of the rather formidable 'good and great' predecessors who chaired the organisation. She was born across the border in High Wycombe in Buckinghamshire. "My parents, Tom and Lucy Spencer ran a pub, The Bell in Frogmore, and it's still there. When I was seven, my father bought a shop in Folkestone. After he sold that, we moved to Harrow, and he worked for a while as a stage hand at the BBC. His most memorable job was backstage on Frankie Vaughan's The Green Door. He had to look through the letter box so all you could see of him was his eyes. He wanted to get back into the pub trade and when I was fourteen, he became the landlord of The Rose in Denmark Street in Wycombe."

Pauline attended High Wycombe High School and left, aged sixteen to join the Civil Service working for the Ministry of Pensions and National Insurance.

"My daughter Sarah was born in 1966 when I was nineteen. I decided to share a house with another lady who had children so that we could help each other. I returned to work but this time, to the private sector, employed by a furniture making company. Wycombe was famous for furniture making but since then the factories have closed. The style of the furniture we produced was 1960s psychedelic rather than traditional. But I worked in the accounts office because I love figures."

"I met my first husband Don Putnam when he arranged a party for a friend. I knew his friend Archie because he had a garage opposite The Rose and was a regular in the pub. Archie had experienced a sad divorce followed by a breakdown and Don wanted to help him start to socialise again. I was invited to that party. At the time I wasn't aware that Archie fancied me but Don was quicker off the mark. We started going out and married in 1974. Don died of cancer in 1981 when I was only thirty-four."

Pauline married Archie in 1983 and she showed me a picture of her with both her husbands: a possible castaway item. "Don was an important part of both of our lives so it worked well. We could talk about him without any jealousy. Don and I had bought a house in Naphill and after we married, Archie moved in with me. In 1989, we bought this house in Wendlebury. Archie owned a motor cycle garage in High Wycombe and it wasn't too long a commute down the M40."

A venture to the village hall...

Pauline continued, "I didn't know anyone in Wendlebury until one winter night I wandered down to the Village Hall for a Wendlebury WI meeting. I felt some trepidation as I walked down that dark road because I was alone and knew none of the members. Someone met me at the door saying, 'Are you the speaker? ' I replied 'No, but I might be a new member.' Immediately they were so welcoming and invited me to their events. I wasn't made to feel like an outsider. "

"At that first meeting I didn't even know that Wendlebury WI was part of this nationwide dynamic network. I could not have imagined that I would help out with the Federation, speak in public or be presented to the Queen. All that mattered at that moment in my life was that the WI was friendly and through it I have made lots of friends."

"Oxfordshire is a particularly active federation which organises a variety of trips and events including to the theatre. There is a lot to be said for an all-female society. It gives shy women the confidence to engage in activities. It certainly gave me confidence. Without the WI I would never have had the opportunities I have had over the years. Wendlebury has made a new banner to mark the centenary so that has to be a nostalgic possibility for Oxtopia."

The WI in action

Pauline's voluntary career with the WI gives an idea of its democratic structure and how the organisation works. She said:

"Within a couple of years I was secretary on the Wendlebury committee and not long after that I was elected Branch President. An accidental tick on a form indicated that I was prepared to be more involved. As a result, I was asked to join the Oxfordshire Federation Year Book Committee. It compiles a list of recommended speakers and organises twice yearly auditions of potential speakers."

This writer is currently on that list in their *Year Book* offering to talk about *Oxford Castaways*. I experienced one of those auditions mistakenly expecting to speak for fifteen minutes to ten people but addressed an audience of 110! Almost all the branches had sent a representative and they all mark their preferences out of the eight speakers they invite to audition. That size of audience is now small fry to Pauline.

"The largest audience I have addressed was of 4,500 at the National AGM in Leeds when I spoke on the resolution to support the Air Ambulance."

In the meantime, Pauline had trained as an accountant. "In 1974, I had been running the accounts department of the Slater Tool Company Ltd. when their auditors head-hunted me. I left the company with their blessing as Slater were experiencing difficulties owing to the three-day week. When in the 1990s, the WI learned of my experience, I was nominated to be a trustee on the County Finance Committee and was elected as treasurer."

Because of her professional experience, Pauline was able to streamline the operation. She said:

"I served as treasurer from 1999 until 2003 when I was elected Federation Chairman. You have to be elected every year. Most serve for three to four years so, in 2009, after six years in the post I resigned. Sue Cox took over for the following four years. When her successor dropped out after only ten months, as an experienced Chairwoman, I was voted in to cover the last two months. And that was how I ended up being elected to serve as Chairwoman in this amazing centenary year."

Centenary celebrations

We talked about the special events organised locally and nationally in 2015. Inspired by the journey of the Olympic Torch, the WI made a special centenary baton that went on a journey around the country. Pauline said:

"It was passed around every Federation within England and Wales. Oxfordshire took it over from Berkshire at the Matthew Pincett Rowing Club. The Oxford Mail photographed our handover to Buckinghamshire in Oxford on April 15. Each Federation has chosen twelve pictures from the relay around their county to be placed inside the baton. We chose photographs of the handovers, the cake cutting at Dorchester Abbey and scenes from its journey through Oxfordshire including by Salter's Steamer down the Thames to the parade in The High."

The banner's last stop was at the Royal Albert Hall where the centenary AGM was held. Two coach loads of delegates went from Oxfordshire to that meeting on June 4 and there was also a representative for each branch at the special Royal Garden Party. As Chairwoman of the Oxfordshire Federation, Pauline was invited into the Royal Tent to meet the Duchess of Cambridge.

Jambusters

The WI has also had its profile raised at least indirectly by the TV series *Home Fires* which was inspired by *Jambusters, the Story of the WI* by Iffley resident Julie Summers. Julie has been a speaker on WI history at Denman College and she told me:

"What impressed everyone involved in the TV series is how brilliantly the WI stepped up to the plate when war came. Unpaid, unsung, to a large extent uncomplaining, these women quietly and often with humour, made the countryside tick. The role of the WI was crucial in two ways: first, the government relied on its links with the National Federation of Women's Institutes to make direct requests of countrywomen to look after evacuees, collect everything from National Savings to bones for the munitions industry and to care for the nation's larder; secondly, the WI at institute level offered women a safety valve." That echoes Pauline's more recent story.

The WI today

You could also say that Pauline's story represents the triumph of the new WI that features in *Home Fires*. "The WI branches are vastly different. If you visit your local branch and don't quite like it's style there is nothing to stop you setting up a new WI."

"The Oxfordshire Federation offers financial and other support to help get the new branch off the ground and then steps back. Sometimes one of our more established WIs needs help when there is a shortage of people willing to sit on the committee. Any association is nothing without its leader and all 142 presidents are valued by their WI community and by the community at large."

If *Home Fires* (of which more series are planned) proves anywhere near as popular as *Call the Midwife*, then perhaps it will help swell the ranks of the WI and see new branches formed as Pauline predicts.

So would Pauline take her crafted Wendlebury WI banner to Oxtopia?

"The banner should stay where it belongs. I particularly enjoy poetry and drama because I like the spoken word. There are lots of books I could choose but I'll take the complete works of Shakespeare because it will keep me going for a long time on the island. I'll find a quiet place and read it aloud. I enjoy all the words and phrases which have come into the language because of Shakespeare. My bookmark could be a photograph of the two most important men in my life together enjoying a drink!".

Born: 1947

Occupation: Chair of the Oxfordshire WI

Castaway Items: *The Complete Works of Shakespeare*

Original OLE Interview: July 2015

On the book cover:
Richard O. Smith
Town & Clown

OXFORD EXAMINED

R

Richard O. Smith

2016 was the 400th anniversary of the death of Shakespeare, and a character particular to the bard's plays is the clown with a philosophical turn of phrase and a sardonic wit. Through his book and radio writings, Richard O. Smith has a good claim to being Oxford's own modern take on the jester.

Richard is an author, freelance writer for magazines, and joke writer for many well-known comedy programmes including *The Now Show* on BBC Radio 4. The 'O' is Richard's 'rescue ring' to save some sense of identity in the sea of Smiths!

Like many Oxford Castaways his story did not begin in Oxford. "I was born in 1964 in Boston, Yorkshire: the original Boston. The Boston that imprisoned the Pilgrim Fathers. After a few weeks they sailed for Holland but were betrayed by the ship's captain. Eventually they set off in the Mayflower from Plymouth. Arriving with a chance to start afresh in a brand new country, they came up with imaginative new names for their new settlements – Boston and Plymouth!"

"My parents Eve and Jim were school teachers. They met through teaching and remained teachers all their professional life. From my mother's side I have some Dutch ancestry. The Lincolnshire fens which lie below sea level are windswept , uncompromisingly flat with no trees or hedgerows to divert the eye from the huge skies. JMW Turner came to Lincolnshire to paint the skies which have a melancholy feeling. The Dutch in the eighteenth century were expert in engineering as Holland is also below sea- level. They drained the fens and I am descended from one of them."

How to become a comic genius

1: have a lonely childhood.

"As a child I spent a lot of time by myself because we lived outside of the town. I couldn't see another house from my bedroom window and my school was miles away." said Richard.

2: experience rejection.

"My nearest neighbour about half a mile away was a girl named Charlotte. She seemed exotically attractive to me as she came from London. Fate would have it that we waited together for the school bus. One day I plucked up the courage to ask her out. She looked at me. Then, in slow motion, turned her gaze downwards to peer at her shoes and turned around without dignifying my request with a response. Soon after this a 'For Sale' sign went up on her house. The next time I saw her, she was a competitor on *Blankety Blank* on BBC1 being on the receiving end of a humiliation, six raspberry sounds. Her fellow contestants turned away in silence. It felt like karma."

3: Grow up in a place which doesn't rate contemporary comedy.

"*The Young Ones*, the comic equivalent to punk, smashed into my consciousness with a spirit of anarchy. I went to Boston Grammar School but left with no qualifications whatsoever. I can't put all the responsibility on the school so I was surprised when last year they asked me to go back and present the prizes at speech day! It is a much better school now than when I was a pupil the school."

Richard says his first comic influence was not Rik Mayall but Basil Brush. Expecting an affinity to animals, he took a holiday job in a pet shop." You can call me the first Pet Shop Boy."

After leaving school, Richard's first writing job was for *The Lincolnshire Standard*.

Football fanzine

"Two weeks into spicing up the village news with jokes they moved me to Obituaries. On my twentieth birthday I left for a livelier life of London. Timing is everything – in life as well as in comedy. After work on my admin day job I indulged my real passion – football writing in the style of Punk DIY. I had arrived in the vanguard (or possibly van guard) of the Football Fanzine Movement [a blend of fan and magazine, a fanzine, is a non-professional and non-official publication produced by fans]."

"Just as Punk was bursting past the gatekeepers of music, this was the new thing in journalism. Football writing in 1984 consisted of Shoot magazine for kids and badly ghost written auto-biographies. The style was condescending. Football is and was so huge in British culture that I asked myself why there wasn't anything written for discerning adults."

1988 saw a new magazine *When Saturday Comes* and Richard contributed humorous pieces for it.

"Examples of my features were 'Great Own Goals of Our Time' and 'Great Sendings Off'. They became popular. Richard hadn't completely abandoned his roots because he edited *From Behind Your Fences*, the independent Boston United fanzine and his talent as a writer was noticed. In 1992, Richard was presented with the award for National Football Writer of the Year at a ceremony in Edgbaston in Birmingham.

"I was just one of the nominees which included Patrick Collins and Harry Pierson of *The Guardian* so I was completely unprepared when the woman in gold opened the golden envelop and said the award winner was ME. I hadn't prepared an acceptance speech. I think I said something like 'I am currently hovering one hundred feet above the lunar surface.'"

Winning that award brought me a commission to write for *The Independent*. It was about this time that I moved to Oxford and it is one of the better things I have done. I moved to a new city and a new job" and he met his wife Catherine, an Oxford open top bus guide.

Comedy sketches

"I heard Lucy Porter before she was famous and I liked the way she didn't try to hide her intelligence and was a female comic not trying to be a man. In the late nineties comedy was more chauvinistic. I began writing additional material for Lucy and met lots of other comics including Henning Wehn. I am the guy who wrote for them before they were funny."

"After that, I began regularly for BBC Radio 4's 6.30pm slots starting with *The News Quiz*. Early in 2000 *The Now Show* contacted me. They had seen sketches I had written. Writing sketches involves a meeting on Tuesday with the cast. They divide you up and suggest topics. It is anxiety inducing because you have to file the results by the same evening. Doing a series of gags and jokes in isolation won't work. You need emotional investment in the piece. That is what one of my favourite comics, David Sedaris is so good at."

4: Be a good cook and have a thick skin.

"Ever since I began writing for comedy shows I get requests like 'Can you get me a job writing for Dara Ó Briain?' (which Richard has done as well) and questions like 'How do you become a comedy writer?' My answer goes down like a lead balloon not least because I reply 'Be prepared to work for free for ten years,'" said Richard.

"Comedy writing pays less than journalism because there are so many people who want to be comedy writers. It has particular challenges. If you write the lyrics of a song you can perform that song over and over again and nobody minds. That doesn't apply to jokes. The burn up rate for comic material is huge. You have to keep coming up with fresh material. The reactions to comedy can be extreme. The audience either love it or hate it. I'm too sensitive to write sitcom. I stick to the jokes."

I skirted around Richard's sensitivity by asking him what was his best review? He replied,

"Richard O. Smith is the English David Sedaris,' and I'm great fan of Sedaris! John Finemore who writes and performs in Cabin Pressure gave me good advice. He said there are three rules for good comedy writing but they apply to all writing. Number 1, write often, Number 2, re-visit the script often and Number 3, cut often."

Writer's (financial) block

So that was lessons five and six! Coming up to date Richard said,

"Even when I was comedy writing I had a day job but in 2012, I was made redundant. Now my day job is writing books but that doesn't pay. 90% of royalties are earned by 2% of authors." Go figure as the yanks might say. Oxford author Philip Pullman has warned that professional writers may become a dying breed and Richard was sounding like another of his heroes Christopher Douglas who is the curmudgeonly voice of fictional freelance writer Ed Reardon (On Radio 4).

Nevertheless Richard has accumulated an impressive backlist of humorous books, and has just written an unlikely *Norse & Nordic Oxford* guidebook (with Ann-Turi Ford, in the design style of DK's Eyewitness Travel series). His earlier titles include *Stupid Criminals: As Thick as Thieves* – a fleeting number one on Amazon's humour section and his only non-fiction book not set in Oxford. He wrote *Student Pranks* in 2010 calling it an 'Alternative History of Oxford.' *The Man With his Head in The Clouds* is the story of James Sadler, the son of an Oxford pastry cook and first Englishman to fly, cleverly interwoven with Richard conquering his crippling fear of heights and succeeded in going up in a Sadler-type balloon. Richard showed me a possible island choice, a shaving mug with an illustration of the Robert Brothers' balloon. They were the first men to fly in a hydrogen balloon.

His love of football continues remains untarnished and when we went to Oxford City football ground for the photoshoot, which Richard told me is the oldest football club in Oxfordshire, he added: "When it moved from Grandpont to Marsden, it took the wrought iron gates with it (made by W Lucy & Co Ltd., the last iron foundry in Oxford) and they must be a desert island choice."

Richard O. Smith

Born: 1964

Occupation: Comedy writer and author

Castaway Items: Wrought iron gates (by W Lucy & Co Ltd) at the Oxford City Ground

Original OLE Interview: April 2016

Castaways 3:25 and 3:26

Tish Francis and Kim Pickin

Is Oxford the Hollywood of stories? This dynamic duo certainly believe our city has enriched the imagination of children with its world-famous stories of hobbits, dark materials, and magical tea parties. Together they are on a mission to bring those stories alive through their Story Museum in the heart of the city.

Tish Francis

Tish was born in Henley. Her father Hamish Francis, (who came up to Oxford a linguist and left, post-war, an agriculture MA), managed the Hambleden Estate farm. A combination of the Chilterns, her unusual primary school, and Christmas visits to ice, circus and theatre shows with a Scottish granny in London fuelled Tish's imagination.

"Neither of my parents were religious but my two elder sisters and younger brother and I, attended a catholic convent school at Friar Park, an extraordinary gothic mansion in Henley. A daily uphill half-mile hike took us through huge iron gates, past bluebell woods and strange way markers. It wasn't just the mystery of religion and attendant pageantry that created the atmosphere in that school, it was the building with its secret panels, optical illusions, carved riddles, gargoyles, door knob in the shape of monks' noses, hidden grottos and fantastic grounds. It was later bought by George Harrison – my favourite Beatle! What child's imagination could fail to be inspired!"

"My compulsion for doing up buildings must come from my mother; an artist / farmer who channelled her creativity and ingenuity into transforming a succession of run down houses into comfortable family homes. In 1965 and by then living on a farm near Twyford I followed my sisters Jacqueline and Caroline to board at St Helen's in Abingdon. It wasn't an easy time for the family: in my late teens my father became ill and had to give up his job and the home that came with it."

Tish sang and acted at St Helen's and joined the Young Playhouse Association not knowing what a huge part it would play in her life.

"I saw my first Pinter play on my seventeenth birthday. It was Old Times and starred Dorothy Tutin, Vivian Merchant and Colin Blakely. A light bulb went on. Unlike now, my school didn't know what to do with a girl wanting a career in theatre. There were few courses and little awareness of the different opportunities – besides acting – in the profession."

After A levels and a year working in London and Oxford, instead of heading for RADA, Tish set off for York University to read Social Science.

"I was troubled by the iniquities of the world and for reasons closer to home I also wanted to understand more about mental illness. Drama took a back seat for a while, though I did play Big Nurse in *One Flew Over the Cuckoo's Nest*. During my University years I made trips to the States and Canada – the second time hitchhiking 10,000 miles coast to coast and back. Memories to last a lifetime."

Tish moved to London in 1977 taking up residence with a group of architects, lawyers and community artists in a 'licensed squat' in Vauxhall and joined the Vauxhall Community Theatre Company.

"We performed shows about Windscale, homelessness, joblessness and founded the Vauxhall City Farm – still flourishing I'm pleased to see."

Then Tish moved to London came across the Covent Garden Community Association – the organisation behind the fight to save the area from the planners' bulldozers. Starting as a volunteer she became its co-ordinator for three years and described it as "a fascinating and vibrant time politically, on the cultural scene and in terms of neighbourhood renewal and community action – a baptism of fire."

"It was around this time my sister Caroline moved to Australia. Planning to visit her for an extended stay, I left the Covent Garden job but, before heading down under, I worked on the founding of the Almeida Theatre in Islington, with three Oxford graduates who had acquired the lease. One of them, Will Bowen was and is a close friend of Kim's and is now a Story Museum Trustee.

"Exhausted and needing a break I took off but almost didn't as I nearly missed my plane. I went to Heathrow when I should have been at Gatwick! I had used up all my savings buying a non-returnable ticket. Thanks to a quick witted friend I was bundled onto a Gatwick bound helicopter; they were closing the cabin doors as I ran up the boarding tube!"

"Returning from Oz nine months later, I became manager of GRAEAE Theatre the UK's first professional company of actors with physical disabilities. I moved them into The Diorama in Regent's Park and produced seven shows including a tour to India – another huge learning curve. The highlight was Mrs Gandhi's attendance at our Delhi performance; unusually she stayed for the whole show and met the company.

In 1985 the director of Shared Experience asked Tish to find the group a home – this was the start of the Soho Laundry Project.

"I cut a deal with Westminster City Council. If I raised the money to refurbish this old municipal laundry they would give us a lease at a low rent," said Tish. Once the Soho Laundry was up and running, Tish met two people who would be important in her life.

"In the 1980s I rekindled my love of swing music at a great London club called the 2 i's. After a Time Out jive contest there, I was invited to teach sessions at Hackney's Chats Palace. One of those I taught (reluctantly I suspect!) was my partner Douglas, now a defence aerospace analyst."

Oxford Playhouse

The Laundry brought Tish together with Hedda Beeby who joined Shared Experience. A couple of years later, with Tish now adding companies like Opera Factory and the Geoffrey Museum to her client list, Hedda joined her small enterprise. Tish said:

"We were originally approached for advice on the appointment of a Director for Oxford Playhouse by Hedda's previous boss who was on the board. Then she suggested we together be put forward 'as a wild card' for the post. The interviews took place on a depressing autumn day – leaves were blowing down St Giles and we were interviewed by a team of twelve."

But they got the job, and in 1989 Tish was appointed joint director with Hedda Beeby to mastermind the major fundraising campaign to re-open, re-programme and refurbish Oxford Playhouse after a four-year closure. As in London, raising the money and overcoming obstacles took humour, diplomacy and dogged determination.

"Looking back we lived on sheer adrenalin and everyone worked together fantastically."

Tish became the sole director from 2001–2008 making her the theatre's longest-serving director. Her original team of two grew to a staff of more than forty. Under her direction the theatre staged over eighty shows annually and stayed opened for all but two weeks of the year.

Her favourite-fateful Oxford Playhouse moments include "a bomb scare on a first night, Judi Dench and Ian McKellen at the opening Gala, seven plays starring Toby Jones and Jason Watkins. Brilliant actors, the brilliant director Doug Hodge and Harold Pinter himself, who flicked that switch in 1971, writing me a personal note of thanks for the 'best ever production of *Dumb Waiter*' and my wonderful send off by the team. Beyond imagining!"

Tish was the executive producer of Oxford's memorable millennium festival OOMF! which exceeded all expectations. With festival manager Rosemary Richards, and festival director Jeremy James and a fabulous team from the community including Oxford Castaways Euton Daley (then with Pegasus Theatre) and Nic Morbath (then at the Zodiac), she set up OOMF! A crowd of over 40,000 people packed into Oxford's South Park for the stunning finale to that *Oxford Millennium Festival*. The event featured choreographed processions, breath-taking pyrotechnics, aerial artistry, and the construction of three new spires for Oxford.

Tish was made a Deputy Lieutenant of Oxfordshire and awarded an Honorary Degree of Arts by Oxford Brookes University and looked forward to a less hectic life with more time for her son James and family.

"The last thing I expected was to be involved in another building project – certainly not in Oxford. But my friend the children's playwright David Wood linked me up with Kim at the now closed QI club. Kim asked 'Didn't you get the email I sent when you left the Playhouse?' I hadn't received it. She then explained her vision and what she needed to take it forward. It was so compelling it was one of those 'has to happen' moments. That fateful meeting brought me here to Rochester House and The Story Museum."

"This project is characterised by Kim's fantastic leadership, our great team (paid and voluntary) and a lot of fairy dust – we have had such a positive response. We need around £8 million to complete the transformation of the whole building. The first phase is nearing completion and we now have a book shop and themed café."

Kim Pickin

Kim was born in Windsor and attended a convent school from the age of four until she left aged seventeen.

"I learned how to wear white gloves at school and not to eat in the street. In contrast, at home, I lived a happy outdoor childhood. My father was from the fifth generation of a boat business on the Thames. Windsor Boats is rather like Salters in Oxford. I grew up helping on the steamers making and serving sandwiches, selling ice cream and dealing with customers. My brother Mark has gone on to run the family business."

"There were not a lot of books in our house because my mother, Janet, was dyslexic. I discovered books at school and each Christmas when I was given £1 I spent it on eight Puffin paperbacks, which I eked out for as long as I could."

When Kim saw a documentary about a small boy called Michael Cooper who ended up in juvenile detention for setting fire to things, it sparked an interest in child psychology.

"No one in my family had been to university and my school didn't push for us to apply. I had read about Oxford and applied independently to St Anne's to read psychology and physiology. I was lucky to be given a place in 1976."

"When looking for a career in the field I was disillusioned to discover than child psychology in those days seemed to be all about controlling children, often with drugs, rather than exploring more creative and positive options. I didn't like what I saw and so applied for a secretarial job at Blackwell Publishers while I thought what to do next."

That proved to be fortuitous because the man she went on to marry in 1987, Robert Faber, was completing his PhD here in Oxford.

"I became a commissioning editor and enjoyed publishing in philosophy and social science for five years. One book I'm particularly proud of was by Jonathan Porritt and this led to me joining the board of Friends of the Earth and developing a life-long interest in sustainability and the environment."

"But after five years I knew I didn't want to work in academic publishing all my life so I went to London Business School in 1986to take an MBA. Two years later I joined Wolff Olins, a branding company as a consultant and writer. For five years I was involved in exciting international projects but by the time my first son Felix was two, I was finding the travel too much. At the same time, in 1993, Robert was given a post at OUP overseeing the huge Oxford Dictionary of National Biography. So I decided to go freelance and we moved back to Oxford."

This gave Kim an idea for her desert island choice. "If I took that multi-volume set I'd have 59,000 life stories to read. There's a lifetime of reading in there and I had the pleasure of watching it grow from a seed to winning the Queen's Anniversary award for OUP. It represents fourteen years of my husband's life."

Robert and Kim had two more sons, Tom in 1993 and Jono in 1997.

"One of my branding jobs was for British Telecom thinking about 'Britishness' and what Britain means to the world. It brought home to me how important literature and language are to our culture – and children's stories are among the most loved things Britain has given the world." said Kim.

"This was re-enforced in my family life. Reading books at bedtime to my three sons was my favourite part of the day. Stories can be incredibly powerful. It's a wonderfully intimate thing to read a story to a small child and see how it develops their language, imagination and empathy, and helps them make sense of the world."

"I began to think there should be somewhere in this country which celebrates children's literature and the power of storytelling. I talked to people about the idea of a Story Museum, initially imagining that someone else would take it up and run with it.

"When Oxford applied to be Capital of Culture, I was introduced to John Lange, then Director of the Museum of Oxford. John had considered creating an Alice in Wonderland gallery. We started working together and, in 2005, we announced to the world our wish to create a story museum in Oxford. I knew Tish had lots of experience developing buildings and so emailed her but had no reply."

Keys to a secret story

We had arrived at that fateful meeting in the QI club and Tish ready to weave her side of the story with Kim's. In May 2009, her main task was to find a suitable site – not exactly easy in Oxford. While Tish was doing that Kim developed outreach projects and spoke to potential funders. Rochester House was once part of the central post office and telephone exchange, and Tish got wind that it was not going to be part of a proposed development for the area.

"We were able to buy it with the help of a generous donor but it was the Soho Laundry over again only more so. We had to make the building habitable," said Tish.

"The day we moved in to bring the building to life we told a story. I was handed a bunch of 183 keys and sent volunteers around the building to see what doors they would open. There are still two enormous safes we haven't seen inside."

Kim and Tish describe the completion of part of the building with the help of an Arts Council grant as 'the end of Chapter One'.

The Story Museum is a place of dreams. I asked what are Tish and Kim's dream items for the island? Tish said "I love amber – full of legends, trapped time and memories of Suffolk beachcombing as a child and now with Douglas – perhaps I can be wearing my amber beads when you maroon me? One of my favourite books is Tove Jannsen's *Moomin Summer Madness*. There's a great flood and the characters are set adrift on their own adventures until some of them come across a floating theatre and it draws them back together. Maybe I could take a theatre?"

"The great thing about being a castaway is that I'll have time to read the complete works of Shakespeare. I'd also like to learn to draw and still have some of my late mother's art pencils but would need some paper."

Kim would also like to take books: "I wouldn't want to leave behind my copies of Philip Pullman's *His Dark Materials*. I read it myself and then aloud to each of my sons: it blew us away. The books would remind me of my sons and Philip Pullman manages to make Oxford the centre of the universe. They bring together many of the things I care about: young people exploring the different worlds of truth and imagination, fact and fiction, right and wrong, and discovering what it means to be human. And this is what lies at the heart of the Story Museum."

Tish Francis

Born: 1954

Occupation: Director, The Story Museum

Castaway Items: Tove Jannsen's *Moomin Summer Madness*

Kim Pickin

Born: 1958

Occupation: Director, The Story Museum

Castaway Items: Philip Pullman's *His Dark Materials* trilogy

Original OLE Interview: April 2014

Paul Hobson

Just down the road from the Story Museum (run by our previous Castaways) lies Modern Art Oxford (MAO). Paul Hobson has come a long way from 'philistine' beginnings in Yorkshire to become its latest director.

In 2016 MAO celebrated its fiftieth anniversary with a look back at its past as well as showcasing some new work. Over 700 exhibitions have been presented at MAO since the gallery was founded fifty years ago. And Paul has the enviable task of welcoming back some artists and work from the past including work by an artist who inspired Paul to a career in visual arts.

As an undergraduate reading history at Brasenose College, Paul first walked through the door into MAO in 1991, when the gallery was exhibiting work by iconoclastic British artist John Latham. Latham died in 2006 so was not aware of the effect he had on Paul's young and curious mind: "I was baffled and confused by Latham's idea of what art is." Paul loved theatre and performance so the work of John Latham, who was influential in developing the idea of event-related art, got him thinking how he could work in the visual arts.

"I was born in Yorkshire in 1970 and educated in Worcestershire. My parents Carol and Alan were both consultants in the health service. Despite being somewhat philistine when it came to the visual arts, they encouraged my sister Lisa and I in all our creative pursuits. My grandfather had a big influence on me. Like most people from his background at that time, he left school aged fourteen. I often wonder what he could have achieved if he had more opportunities in life. He was musically gifted and played several instruments, which he taught himself. Music was a constant feature of the household and influential on my sister learning to play the cello. He encouraged me to share his love of the arts and I did: I joined art societies and took part in amateur dramatics. I even wrote plays and one of them was produced by The National Youth Theatre."

"My 'A' levels were in English, History, Art and Economics. I enjoyed fine art drawing and considered applying to art school but pragmatism won the day because I chose to read history which I considered a versatile subject."

"Once I had discovered MAO as student in Oxford, I saw lots of shows over the years and began seriously to consider how I could work in the visual arts. I realised that with such a non-vocational degree I needed to take an MA which would enable me to find an entry-point job in the art world. I did an MA in Arts Management and Policy at City University."

He was being modest because he has three MAs, which make him well qualified for the leadership post at MAO.

From the Hayward to the Serpentine galleries

"My first post in the field was as a researcher at the Hayward Gallery between 1993 and 1995. The idea of Cool Britannia was emerging. I headed for the Royal Academy in 1996 and worked there until 2000. It was an amazing experience and I have huge affection for the RA. It strengthened my growing interest in contemporary art."

From there he became head of strategy at the Serpentine Gallery in Hyde Park in 2000. Paul continued,

"A very different and in many ways privileged professional experience was working for a private charitable foundation supporting new commissions of art. It wasn't just for the traditional visual arts but for contemporary poetry, dance companies and experimental performances too. One of the most memorable was a new Artangel commission by Francis Alys which the foundation supported, in which a fox was released at night in the National Portrait Gallery and filmed on CCTV as it made its fugitive way through the Elizabethan and Jacobean galleries... It could also be frustrating because there was never enough money to support many amazing projects."

"After the foundation, I was interim director of a tiny East London gallery in Bethnal Green called The Showroom Gallery, which I loved! The roof leaked and we kept sandbags in the office that were constantly sprouting mushrooms in more clement weather, but it was inspirational. With the help of an intern I worked with up and coming artists early in their careers who I thought would make a difference. I've been really fortunate to have worked in very different organisations during my twenty year career."

Paul's last post before coming to Oxford was as director of the Contemporary Art Society. Under his leadership, the Society strengthened its programmes and profile leading to an unprecedented period of growth. His knowledge learned both academically and in the 'real' world in so many different organisations were a great preparation for leading MAO at a difficult time.

Paul took up the post in September 2013. "My first year in the post was one of stabilising and reassuring an organisation traumatised by the unexpected death of his predecessor at MAO, Michael Stanley" [also an Oxford Castaway].

'A free gallery bringing education and inspiration'

"I think I was appointed in recognition of the fact that I can give vision and direction, whilst balancing the books. MAO is part-funded by Arts Council England and the local authority, it is essential in these lean times to balance the books, be accountable and be as accessible as possible. Times are quite hard for most people, so free recreational activities can be what make life worth living. People want inspiration and to have somewhere of the standing of Modern Art

Oxford on the doorstep, a free gallery that brings education and inspiration, is especially valuable."

Paul relishes the challenge of connecting with hard-to-reach audiences and says. "If you value and don't underestimate your audiences, people can and will get challenging contemporary art."

MAO is one of the most important contemporary art spaces in the UK with an international reputation for its exhibitions, projects and commissions. Where does Paul intend to take MAO in the future?

"In the years ahead we will begin a programme of work on the building, which needs quite a lot of work, and this will improve the visitor experience."

Paul also plans many changes to the programme and the way Modern Art Oxford is run.

"We might think it quite odd in the years to come that we have this notion of art where people go into galleries and look at things on plinths, because it's quite a 20th-century thing to do. Audiences today are looking at visual information, on the Internet, in social media and they're producing content themselves. Put that alongside all the other different things artists are doing that are away from galleries like this and I'm interested in how a physical space like MAO responds to those trends in culture."

"I will build upon the amazing history of exhibition-making here but there's another opportunity to engage with the different things artists are doing. Contemporary art practice has become diverse and lots of artists are doing things away from white-cube spaces so we also need to engage in reaching out into the community."

We hadn't talked much about Paul's castaway art and objects but he was pretty sure about what he wopuld take to Oxtopia. "I have a Limited Edition portrait by Francis Bacon and I love it. I wouldn't want to be without that!"

Paul Hobson

Born: 1955

Occupation: Director of Modern Art Oxford

Castaway Items: Limited Edition portrait by Francis Bacon. Art in Theory 1900–2000: An Anthology of Changing Ideas (1992) by Charles Harrison and Paul Wood

Original OLE Interview: July 2016

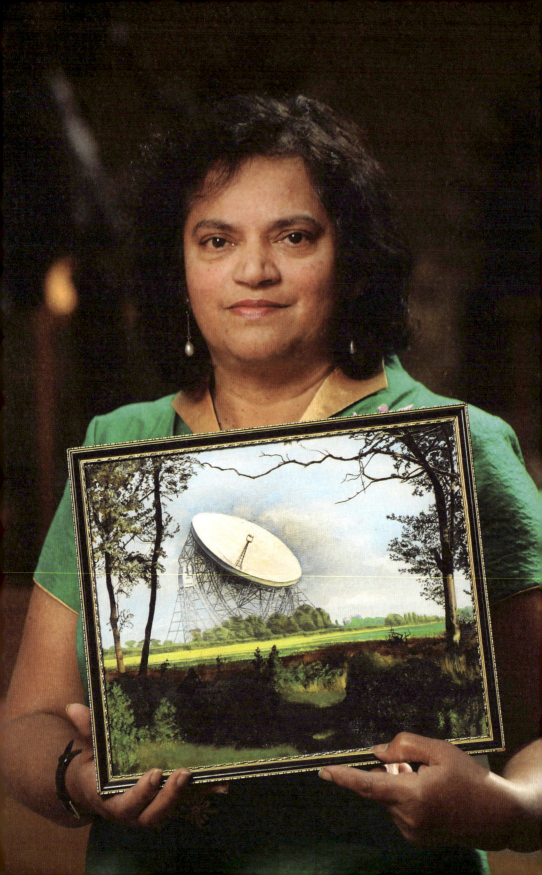

Yasmin Robson

She is an astrophysicist who has had a remarkable, not to say, challenging journey to Oxford considering that her ancestors were indentured labourers at the tail end of slavery.

Yasmin Daniels was born in British Guiana, now known as Guyana, the only English speaking country in South America. She believes that her ancestors came from the Lucknow area of North India to work as agriculture labourers in the British colony, in return for a passage back to India or a plot of land on which to settle at the end of a five-year contract. While those ancestors chose to stay put, travel was obviously in the blood as several generations later, her parents set off for the mother country.

"I arrived in London with my family at the age of three and apart from a few years at St Joseph's Mercy High School in Guyana, where I did my London Board GCE O-Level exams, I have lived in Britain for most of my life. In 2005 I took my husband (David Robson) and sons to visit Guyana for the first time. I had not been there for thirty-three years. It is undeveloped and has pristine rainforest. We took a tiny plane to visit the spectacular Kaieteur Falls, one of the most powerful waterfalls in the world. With a single drop of 226m, it is roughly four times higher than Niagara Falls and not a person in sight."

Yasmin studied at University College Cardiff where she specialised in applied mathematics and astronomy.

"Straight after graduating in 1977, I went to the Royal Greenwich Observatory (then based in Sussex) and was really excited to live and work at Herstmonceux Castle. I had a glorious time there, analysing data and getting up to a lot of pranks – we were told that it was expected of us. We 'sacked' many of the astronomy staff and put the Castle up for sale! We got a far better offer for it than it was eventually sold for years later when the observatory moved home. I also met my future husband, a fellow student, David there."

Tuning in to radio astronomy

"I was fascinated to learn about the Cosmic Microwave Background radiation, an echo of the Big Bang, and decided that I wanted to be a Radio Astronomer. I felt I needed more practical experience, so I got a job in industry with GEC Marconi Research Laboratories in Chelmsford as an Antenna Research Engineer. This involved designing aerials for geo-stationary satellite communications, including an antenna for the Goonhilly Downs Earth Station on the Lizard in Cornwall."

In 1983 Yasmin gained her Doctorate in Radio Astronomy at the Jodrell Bank Observatory where her work involved neutral Hydrogen observations and examining stability and missing mass in groups of galaxies.

"While I was a PhD student at Jodrell, I sent a postcard of the Lovell telescope to my friend, Steve Eborall (from Marconi's) who was laid up in hospital with a broken leg. From his bed he used the postcard to paint a beautiful picture of the telescope for me. It brings back wonderful memories of my time there and would be a castaway item for me."

"I loved spending many weeks at a time using the Lovell Telescope, including clambering up to the focus box way up high to change bits of the telescope. Jodrell was isolated so we had to make our own fun and I could often be found playing cricket at lunchtime during the summer."

"I trekked into Manchester for choir and concerts." She has a passion for music and always sung in choirs and it was during this Yasmin won an award (which still amuses her family today): "I was pronounced 'Bounciest Bathing Belle' in Pirates of Penzance for my performance with Manchester University Gilbert and Sullivan Society (MUGSS)!"

'Oxbridge'

In 1984, David and Yasmin married and moved to Cambridge where he held a fellowship in astronomy.

"In those days it was impossible to get two posts in astronomy at the same establishment so I worked for Cambridge Interactive Systems as a software engineer programming 3D computer graphics before taking a career break to raise three sons – Daniel, Darius and Duncan. We lived in a mobile home in Cambridge with two babies as it was a struggle to find places to rent that would take children, and house prices were going through the roof."

"We moved to Oxford when Darius was six months old. When Duncan started school I managed to get work as an Associate Lecturer for the Open University, teaching Astronomy and Planetary Science in Reading. I heard about a scheme to help scientists return to research following a career break and was successful in gaining a Daphne Jackson Fellowship in the Astrophysics Department at University of Oxford as well as a Fellowship at St Hilda's College."

"Daphne Jackson was the first female professor of physics in the UK. She felt it was a waste of resources and skills that women who had had children were unable to find work in science suited to their qualifications and were reduced to

taking low-level jobs. She set up the Daphne Jackson Trust to help women return to their science. The scheme has now helped over 250 scientists (male and female) and I was fortunate to be among them."

In 1999, Yasmin took up a Research Fellowship at the Cavendish Laboratories at the University of Cambridge, working on the development of an international collaboration – the ALMA Telescope. She participated in a site-testing campaign in the Chilean Andes at 5,000m above sea level, in the Atacama Desert, one of the driest places on Earth and where the telescope has now been built. Yasmin then showed me some stunning photographs of the Andes which are possible choices to take to Oxtopia.

"I gave a paper of my analysis at the International Astronomical Union conference in Marrakesh and represented the UK in a multi-national collaboration during site-testing and analysis of the atmosphere in Chile, including launching Helium balloons. It was certainly challenging to function at that altitude without additional oxygen."

Women in science

Yasmin began to fulfil her dreams of working as an astrophysicist, but she was acutely aware of the hurdles faced by all working women wanting to take career break to be a mothers – and wanted to do something to bring those hurdles down.

"More recently my work has involved supporting women scientists and striving to achieve a cultural step change to enable women to raise their family as well as participate in science research and technology. Up to now everything has been about 'fixing' the women so that they fit into a male environment. The European Platform of Women Scientists is trying to bring about change in policy, requiring reform to be made by the institutions themselves."

An early example of a woman scientist who also brought up a family is Oxford crystallographer, Dorothy Hodgkin, the first British woman to receive a Nobel Prize for science. Yasmin's fellow resident of Oxtopia, Georgina Ferry (3:10) has written a biography of Dorothy and it is clear how dedicated and determined she had to be to succeed in a man's world.

As well as coordinating the annual Dorothy Hodgkin Memorial Lecture, Yasmin is on the organising committee of the Oxford International Women's Festival which takes place in March to celebrate women's achievements and to highlight the challenges faced worldwide. She is also Treasurer for Oxford Association for Women in Science and Engineering and has contributed to a paper entitled How to Combine Physics and a Family.

Yasmin also continues her passion for promoting music and is on the Board of Trustees of the Friends of The Young Musicians Association which supports young musicians in and around Oxfordshire with their music education.

"My sons have enormously enjoyed their years with Central Music School and Oxfordshire County Youth Orchestra and I am a firm believer that music is an excellent way for young people to channel their creative energies."

"Throughout my life I've belonged to at least one choir at any one time, sometimes three! I've had no formal music training unlike my three sons who play several instruments and all learned piano with Trevor Cowlett completing their Grade 8 with him and one going on to study music at university." Trevor (Castaway 3:29) is the Director of Kennington United Choirs and although Yasmin lives in Headington she sings with his choir. "Singing has been a constant in my life since the choir at John Burns Primary School in Battersea. Now I sing a mixture of serious pieces interspersed with Gilbert & Sullivan's operettas giving me an excuse to dress up in costume."

I asked Yasmin what her castaway wishes would be: "I can't imagine not having any novels to read and would love to take the complete works of Jane Austen with me. I enjoy her character analyses and it would keep me entertained. It looks as though I will be sharing the island with other castaways, so we could probably swap books and set up a choir when we're not building shelters and finding food. But if I can only take one thing, it would have to be my snorkelling gear as I would be keen to explore the clear turquoise waters, coral reefs and spectacular coloured fish."

Yasmin Robson

Born: 1955

Occupation: Astrophysicist

Castaway Items: Snorkelling gear; complete works of Jane Austen; painting of Jodrell Bank

Original OLE Interview: June 2016

Castaway 3:28

Richard Bruce Parkinson

Oxford's Griffith Institute holds the complete original excavation records of Howard Carter who famously discovered Tutankhamun. Richard Bruce Parkinson is a director there and calls it the 'Scotland Yard of Egyptology'. As a Professor of Egyptology he is also something of a detective inspector himself.

The Griffith Institute is tucked away in a wing of the Sackler Library just behind the Ashmolean in St John's Street and a few years back The Ashmolean celebrated the Griffith Institute's 75th anniversary with an exhibition called *Discovering Tutankhamun*. Most of the exhibits demonstrated the meticulous manner in which Howard Carter and his team photographed and described their unbelievable finds.

The mysteries that Richard has investigated may surprise some readers because many involve poetry. It should not really be a revelation that an ancient culture which created such beautiful art also wrote beautiful words. That poetry and the beauty of the hieroglyphs inspired the eleven-year old Richard and led to his intriguing career.

Richard was born in Teesdale, County Durham, the only child of two teachers. His mother, Jessie, taught home economics. "She'd wanted to study history but when she was growing up academic choices for women from her background were limited. My father, Harold Parkinson, was an artist, and because he'd been interested in Egypt as a child, I grew up surrounded by art books on the subject and was struck by the beauty of Egyptian script."

"I went to Barnard Castle School, and an inspirational English teacher, Alan Wilkinson (who happened to have studied at The Queen's College, Oxford) sparked a passion in me for literature. I can remember the precise moment in class when I asked myself how poetry works. My two schoolboy enthusiasms collided in the masterpiece of Ancient Egyptian poetry, The Tale of Sinuhe, and I became aware that poetry need not be modern or European. In this poem the hero tells how his life journey took a wrong turn; it's a sort of portrait of a voice trying to find itself. That appeals to me and would be a castaway choice."

"I would also take dad's drawing of Tutankhamun's tomb, done to teach me measured perspective as a schoolboy in 1978. It was based on material from the Griffith Institute, where it now hangs, and it was included in the Discovering Tutankhamun exhibition, which would have delighted him."

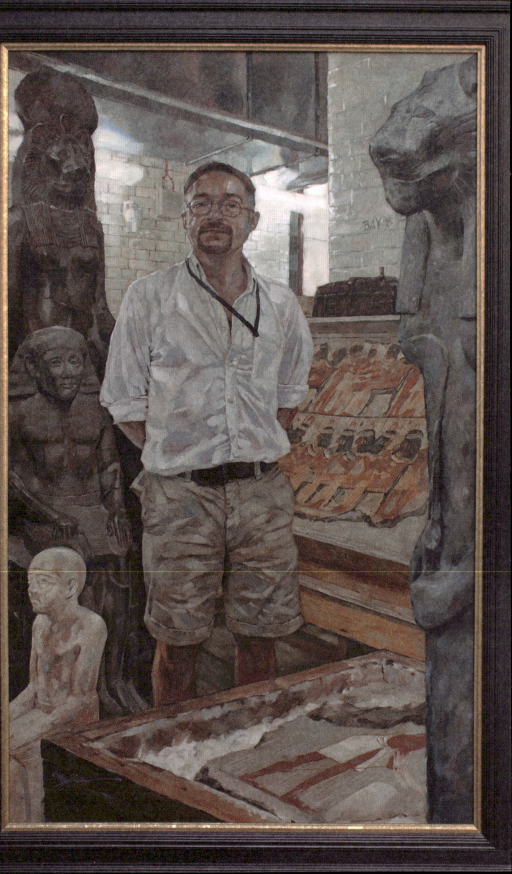

The curse of *The Tale of Sinuhe*

The young Richard was not attracted to Egyptology by mummies, gold and curses but by something much more human and deeper. But this came with a cost: aged thirteen he was in his mother's living room using red ink to copy out the hieroglyphs of The Tale of Sinuhe. "I clumsily spilled the ink onto the new carpet. My parents were not particularly well off and I'll never forget my mother's horror and grief. She nobly kept her temper, we tried to clean it as much as we could, and then moved the settee to hide the stain."

Richard studied English, French, Latin and Art at 'A' level and applied to read Egyptology at The Queen's College, Oxford which has a long association with the subject. He graduated with a first in 1985. But he told me that during his time as an undergraduate at the university he sometimes felt like an outsider:

"I was very happy, but sometimes Oxford seemed to be really intended for people who were white, male, heterosexual, rich and privileged (and southern). My father never visited me in Oxford; I think he worried that his northern accent would be an embarrassment. And I felt culturally and socially marginal in the way many young gay people do, and I felt far too stupid to do anything worthwhile or useful (I still feel that). A friend and I would always joke about the 'Great Social Event To Which We Were Not Invited'. Remembering these feelings, I thought twice about returning to work here, but it's been marvellous to come back to the Institute and especially to Queen's, which is an immensely supportive and welcoming place. My only problem is that as I walk through the college now I'm never entirely sure whether I'm twenty or fifty, and whether I'm going to bump into old or new friends, or both."

Verses from before Christ

Richard is best known internationally as an expert on the poetry of the classic age (1940–1640 BC) "What I enjoy is the experience of attempting an integrated reading of ancient texts, thinking about their changing contexts, their performance, and their emotional and intellectual impact on their audiences— what they meant for their original audiences and what they can mean now. I'm interested in issues of performance practice, cultural power, and sexuality."

Being in the Egyptian landscape is very important to Richard. "You can't read a poem without knowing the feel of its landscape. But I've been an insulin dependent diabetic since I was eleven, and when I was in Egypt on excavation as a graduate student it all went badly wrong with a 48-hour coma. After that I could never ask another fieldwork team to take me on, but I spend as much time as I can in Egypt, lecturing on Nile cruises whenever possible."

One work of art made a mark on our castaway's life in 1987—the release of the film Maurice, based on the novel of the same title by EM Forster. It is a tale of same sex love in the early 20th century. Richard said, "I was already a great admirer of EM Forster and his advocacy of the 'inner life', and his novels were very important for my own self-awareness. The inner life must always come first. When I saw the Merchant Ivory film, I found it very inspirational—it is wonderfully

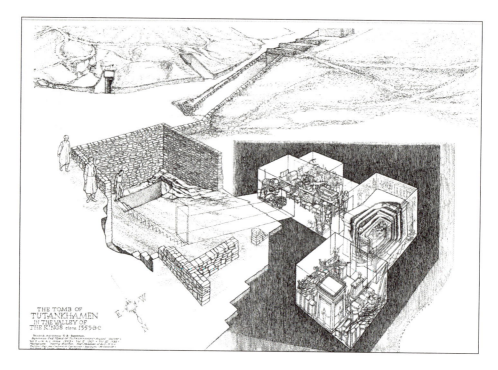

THE TOMB OF
TUTANKHAMEN
IN THE VALLEY OF
THE KINGS circa 1353-B-C

romantic and quietly heroic—and by a strange coincidence I met my husband Tim in Oxford exactly three years to the day later. So I'd want a copy of that on the island."

In 1990, Richard was still in Oxford as a junior research fellow at University College Oxford. "Florence has always been a favourite city, thanks to my father and to Forster—it was the first place I ever travelled on my own, using the advance payment from my first book, and I went there with Tim soon after we met. We privately exchanged rings in Santa Croce—sometimes one has to re-invent rites for oneself. We'd often eat sandwiches in Piazza S Maria Novella under a loggia, and we picked up a small fragment of pietra serena (limestone) which was lying in the gutter. It now sits on the mantelpiece at our flat in North London. That's also a must have for the island, to remind me of all the times in Florence with Tim and all the works of art created with that lovely grey stone from the hills of Fiesole."

Rosetta Stone revealed

In 1991, there was a job opening at the British Museum. "Permanent jobs in Egyptology are few and far between. Part of the job requirements was that the candidate needed to be able to copy inscriptions. I could read hieroglyphs and thanks to Dad I could draw; I ended up with the job and stayed for over twenty years."

That was how Richard became a curator in the Department of Ancient Egypt and Sudan. His academic responsibilities included curating the papyri, as well as inscribed material such as the Rosetta Stone, the iconic key to Egyptian hieroglyphs. Richard said, "On the bicentenary of the discovery of the Stone, we had it conserved and cleaned, and discovered that it wasn't black basalt but grey granite with a pink streak. It was a bit of a shock, but that's what works of arts do. You think you know them, but they always surprise you."

"What I particularly like about the museum world is the emphasis on public service and accessibility, and I enjoy seeing the effect encounters with art have on people, how they can change lives. My biggest project was a permanent gallery with the wall-paintings from the tomb of an official called Nebamun (around 1325 BC). They are very spectacular, and when we placed the fragments together the most beautiful bits of painting often turned out to be at eye level. You can't explain that exclusively through politics or ideology. Perhaps a beautifully painted butterfly is sometimes simply that—a beautiful butterfly. Sometimes academics are, as Raymond Williams said, trained to detachment. What appeals to me is not the abstract and the academic, but the material and the emotional, the touch of the real."

"Working with designers, conservators, museum assistants and performers is such a privilege. That's why my inaugural lecture here, about Sinuhe of course, was accompanied by a great friend, the actress and novelist Barbara Ewing, who can bring insights to a text that an academic like me never can."

Richard was appointed Professor of Egyptology in the Faculty of Oriental Studies full-time in January 2014.

"The idea of a job where I was paid to read texts with students was irresistible, and such an immense privilege. The seventy fifth anniversary was a horrifically exciting time to start, but it's also been a perfect moment to take stock and to consider how to move the subject forward."

'Accessibility is key'

The Griffith Institute houses an archive of wonderful things containing the collective memory and life work of some of Egyptology's greatest scholars, including its founder Professor Francis Llewellyn Griffith. "With this archive we are uniquely placed as a home for Egyptology in Oxford, with the Ashmolean collections next door, and the Sackler (one of the world's greatest Egyptology libraries) — and of course the students. We hope to fully digitise our archive and research resources so that it is accessible free of charge anywhere in the world, especially for scholars and students in Egypt."

"Accessibility is the key thing: when I started in the British Museum, I was told that you had to bear in mind two audiences when writing a label: an eleven-year-old school pupil and a visiting professor from Germany. You had to speak to both simultaneously, and I think it's intellectually very important to write for a diverse and inclusive audience. The Discovering Tutankhamun exhibition was an amazing opportunity to connect the university's research with the public."

Richard took me into the temperature controlled room where the archives are stored and showed me a leather bound album of exquisite watercolours by Howard Carter. Carter copied hieroglyphic signs of birds and then painted the same birds from nature. Surprisingly it is the hieroglyphs that are more animated. So we had gone full circle back to the young Richard copying out Egyptian signs and wrecking the front room carpet.

It was time for him to look at his list for Oxtopia and say which one he would choose if he could only have one. The answer was immediate, "James Ivory's *Maurice* — the inner life must always come first."

Richard Bruce Parkinson

Born: 1963

Occupation: Professor of Egyptology and Director of the Griffith Institute

Castaway Items: DVD of *Maurice* based on the novel of the same title by EM Forster

Original OLE Interview: December 2014

Trevor Cowlett

In the process of becoming the founder and musical director of the Kennington Choir, Trevor Cowlett had to conquer crippling agoraphobia (fear of open or public places) – the toughest call for any choir leader surely?

Trevor Cowlett formed the seventy-strong Kennington and District United Church Choirs (to give it its full name) at the end of 1973. Together since then they have embarked on over forty years of singing for charities, local, national and international raising over £432,000: an amazing achievement for a local amateur choir.

But for thirty years Trevor was a 'prisoner' in his own home a victim of severe agoraphobia. "Sometimes even going into the garden was difficult. I would start sweating and break out in utter panic," he revealed to me. It is thought than one in thirty of us suffer from some form of anxiety. Trevor's story is about his struggle to conquered his phobia so that now he enjoys travelling all over the world playing and teaching music. He can't remember exactly how many young people he has taught but suspects it is well over one thousand.

So where did it all start?

"I was born in Twickenham. There was little music in the family although my father, Albert, belonged to the local philharmonic society. He worked for the Metropolitan Police Orphans Fund and his job was to visit police widows and to make sure they were financially secure. My mother, Elsie, saw it as her job to look after the family including my only sibling – a brother, Douglas, twelve years older than me. We had a piano and I played it as often as I could. At five years of age it was deemed that I should have lessons."

"When the Second World War began, my mother was frightened and declared that we should move to the village of Lane End in the Chilterns, where most of her family lived. There I discovered that I had five aunts and uncles and numerous cousins. My uncle Bern owned a large furniture factory in the middle of the village and I spent hours watching the work and getting in everyone's way."

Popular organ player

Trevor also fell in love with the organ in the Methodist chapel there.

"It was a new two-manual pipe organ with pedal board. They were proud of it and lo and behold one of my aunts was organist. Knowing my interest in the piano she asked if I'd like to try the organ. It was love at first sight. Indeed an organ has to be a priority for Oxtopia. My parents arranged for me to have professional lessons with Owen Hickman, the borough organist of High Wycombe. It wasn't long before I was helping him out with appointments around the town."

"The Congregational Church at Bourne End advertised for a church organist. Owen Hickman suggested I apply and, at the tender age of twelve, I found myself in charge of a goodly-sized pipe organ and a choir of about twenty. Most of our church organists were in the forces so I was in great demand," Trevor recalled.

"When the Americans joined the war and arrived in High Wycombe, many girls were smitten so weddings were popular. I must have played for a wedding in almost every Parish Church in the county! Organists were gold dust. In 1946 approaching my fouteenth birthday I became the organist of Trinity Congregational Church in High Wycombe with a lovely three-manual Father Willis organ and a choir of about thirty."

Trevor passed all his piano exams and everything went well for the precocious young musician until the war ended. His parents returned to London and Trevor, who had won a scholarship to the Royal Grammar School in High Wycombe, became a boarder. That is when his troubles began.

"I gave a short organ recital before the Sunday evening service and came to the attention of a young lady of about my age who sang in the choir and we became friendly. We liked to go shopping on a Saturday afternoon or visit the cinema. I was upset when the school prohibited me, as a boarder, from seeing her saying she would hold up my Oxbridge hopes and that boarders were not allowed out with girlfriends at weekends."

Trevor was a sensitive young man and the bullying experience affected him deeply.

"Pressure was put upon the church and upon my parents to break up the relationship. I was made to quit the church organist post. You can imagine the shock. I was hoping for an Oxbridge music or organ scholarship in a couple of years and the school was not supporting me. I panicked and experienced a combination of agoraphobia and claustrophobia (which has never really left me)."

"The powers that be relented a little (realising that they had made a great mess of things) by allowing me to take a temporary post at Gerrards Cross Parish Church and then at Terriers Parish Church. It was here that my choir was offered two weeks at York Minster to sing while the Minster choir was on holiday. I enjoyed getting to know Francis Jackson, the Minster organist who gave me great encouragement and the freedom of the Minster organ. But my playing had suffered and how I won a place to Oxford I do not know."

"I was lucky to have among my tutors Sir Jack Westrup who was the Heather Professor of Music and a walking encyclopaedia on early Italian opera, which he produced each year in Oxford Town Hall. I studied composition with Dr Bernard Rose who at that time was at The Queen's College. My third tutor was Sir Thomas Armstrong, who was Choragus (choir leader) of Christ Church. A formidable Trinity! But by the time I reached finals, my health had deteriorated and I took exams in the Warneford Hospital where I achieved a sad third."

Trevor's career plans were put on hold but he had one lucky break. He had met Brenda Williams in Twickenham where he spent the vacations.

"Throwing caution to the winds we decided to marry. So it was, on the 23rd July 1955, that the ceremony took place in the Methodist Church in Rose Hill. It was nice and small. I was uncomfortable in large spaces. We moved to a ground floor flat in the Woodstock Road."

"Brenda was a teacher. There was a vacancy at Kennington. She got the job and cycled to work each day. New houses were going up in a road called Bagley Close. One of my uncles came to the rescue and put down the deposit for us and the close became the Cowletts home in May 1956. No sooner had we arrived than David was born at the end of May."

To build a church

"My health seemed to be improving so I applied for the Head of Music position at Larkmead School in Abingdon and got it. I was there from 1957 to 1962 when my health let me down again and I was more or less confined to the house. Peter was born in 1960, and Mary in 1965."

Although the phobia confined him, it didn't stop his ambition. In fact he and a few other villagers had the ambition to build a church.

"We had no money and we had no land. But the determination was there – sales of work, a Saturday morning market stall, selling bricks – everything you can think of. Edith Gandy offered us the paddock at the back of her bungalow in Upper Road where the Church now stands. Planning permission was turned down more than once. But we got the Oxford Methodist Circuit on our side. Synod gave its permission. The Methodist Connexion came up with some funds and we opened on Saturday, October 29th 1967 free from debt."

"Then my health got worse until I got to the point where I couldn't bear Brenda to leave the house. She resigned from Kennington School and we set up a Nursery School in our own home which ran from 1964 right up to 1983. I also gave music lessons at home and still do."

Conducting next to the main doors

In 1973 an ecumenical idea was gaining ground to form a choir made up of members from each of the three Kennington churches. It began with a United Carol Service. Kennington and District United Church Choirs was formed and Trevor was asked to take it on. Its home in the Methodist Church was appropriate since Methodism was born in song. Charles Wesley, the brother of founder John, wrote over 6,000 rousing hymns.

"With my agoraphobia this was hard: I conducted from the main doors from where I could easily escape. I was awash with perspiration but it was a success. People wanted more. Could we do something for Easter? So we gave a performance of Stainer's Crucifixion."

"Our numbers were growing and we had singers from all around Oxford (Radley, Cumnor, Cowley). Could we do some Messiah in the autumn, please? We did but I continued conducting from the main doors. The programme became ever more ambitious and local soprano Sylvia Patterson recruited soloists from Oxford and Abingdon Operatic societies but they needed to restrict their ambitions because Trevor experienced minor anxiety attacks more frequently. Then they became more intense:

"I began to feel an absolute dread of open spaces. I found it difficult to go further than one hundred yards from our home without feeling a tremendous urge to retreat inside. The choir had invitations to sing in Rose Hill, in Witney, Abingdon, Woodstock, Barton; Faringdon; Brill and at the Holywell Music Room. How could I travel to all these places?"

Mini-van to mini Metro to Med cruises

Trevor undertook some behaviour therapy: "It helped me understand the condition but I couldn't overcome it. I didn't meet others who faced the same problem – it was a practical impossibility. Brenda suggested buying a mini-van and making it homelike – an extension of our home. It worked in as much as I stayed inside while Brenda went shopping."

"In 1983, the old van packed up after years of service. We decided to try a smaller car – a Mini Metro. That was the beginning of an about-turn in my feelings. For reasons which I have never been able to explain my feelings of agoraphobia eased. I wanted to travel beyond Kennington and explore. In 1984, we got to the seaside for the first time in nearly thirty years. In 1989, we took the first of our cruises to the Mediterranean. Life had suddenly blossomed and for the first time ever, I experienced real joy and happiness." By 1985, the choir too was able to sing all over the county.

"No-one in the choir is a professional singer. Some have never sung before, some can't read music. But the choir is open to everyone. There are no auditions and believe it or not, no subscriptions. The choir bears all its own expenses. Never is a penny taken from the charity collection. If we're running short of cash, I simply ask and it's always forthcoming." When Brenda sadly died in 1995, the choir rallied around to support Trevor through that difficult time.

Services to music

Trevor also enjoyed a happy seven-year period tutoring sixth-form pupils, but had another set back when he suffered kidney failure and spent seven weeks in hospital. On his return from hospital he found a surprise awaiting him:

"Imagine my delight and unbelief when I got home to find a letter from the Lord Chancellor awaiting me to offer me the honour of the MBE for services to music in Oxford. I accepted, as much as for others as for myself. On Friday, March 2, 2012 I found myself on a thick, foggy morning being driven to Windsor Castle by my son who had spent the night with me. My own three children stood down to allow my three grandchildren to go into the ceremony – something I hope they will never forget. How I wish Brenda could have been there."

"I still have to spend three mornings a week for the foreseeable future on a dialysis machine. So a lot of work had to go and the college work was the main victim. I kept most of my home students and still teach seventy per week."

And the choir? "It is unique in Oxford because we don't have auditions. Anyone who wants to sing can come and join us [astrophysicist Yasmin Robson our previous castaway 3:27 is a choir member]. If in 1973, you would have told me that this amateur untrained choir would one day sing in a college chapel, I would have said 'If pigs could fly.'"

On Oxtopia, he will have many talented musicians to inspire him and they will be delighted with his final choice of object, the Royal Festival Hall organ complete with a generator to power it. If he can't take that then the Exeter College organ will have to do and the complete works of Bach stored in a large organ stool so that he can start a choir on our desert island.

Trevor Cowlett

Born: 1932

Occupation: Choir leader

Castaway Items: Royal Festival Hall organ or the Exeter College organ

Original OLE Interview: April 2015

The full story of the Kennington and District United Church Choirs appears in *I Love You All – The story of Oxford/Kennington choir told in a chorus of voices by Sylvia Vetta* and was launched on Trevor's 83rd birthday

Castaway 3:30

Sylvia Vetta

Our final Oxford Castaway is, fittingly, the person who started it all. Sylvia Vetta invented Oxtopia and the idea of castaways sharing their stories and their skills on an imaginary island. Now the tables are turned on this lady with the legendary powers of persuasion as she finds herself being interviewed by another Castaway (2:25) Philip Hind.

Over the past eight years Sylvia has treated us to 118 Castaway features. Each one neatly encapsulates the life and experiences of someone with a strong connection to Oxford, told in part through the choice of items the subject would take with them to Oxtopia. It is probably quite fortunate that this island exists only in the imagination since most of the objects chosen were very ill suited to the task of building shelters or propagating crops. New arrivals will find little food or shelter, but eclectic and fascinating company and objects.

"It has been such a privilege to interview such inspirational people. I can't think of any other project where the subjects have come from such diverse backgrounds be they 'town', 'gown' or 'county'", says Sylvia.

"What I love about the castaways is that even the famous ones would prefer not to be called 'celebrities'. What I think unites them – apart from their obvious Oxford connection –is their positive and creative attitude to life. They are doers. It is often hard work against the odds that has enabled them to achieve and connect with the world."

Sylvia is a doer extraordinaire! As Castaway Dai Richards (2:5) explains, "She is irrepressible. She just goes for it. She seems always to search out the most worthwhile causes and put her all into them." Artist-castaway Weimin (1:40) agrees: "Sylvia is probably the most energetic person I have ever met!"

Storytelling, creating and sharing opportunities, and helping people to fulfil their potential whatever their circumstances are recurring themes in Sylvia's own story.

She was born in Luton, just after the Second World War, the daughter of Charles, an engineer and Doris who, with her sisters, worked in a corset factory. Her parents' house was newly built and, although she was very young at the time, Sylvia remembered how her mother was chastised by her neighbours for befriending the Italian prisoners-of-war working on nearby roads.

Every Saturday, from the age of seven Sylvia would make a three-mile round trip to Luton Central Library where she developed a love of language and literature that has stayed with her ever since. "I had no guidance about what to read so I just read anything!"

Teaching immigrant children

After Luton High School, Sylvia wanted to join Voluntary Service Overseas but Alec Dickson, the founder of VSO, said that at seventeen she was too young. Instead he suggested she consider joining a new programme of UK-based Community Service Volunteers. So, in 1963 Sylvia went to Smethwick in the West Midlands to teach English to immigrant children.

"Money was very tight, and the accommodation wasn't very good…and the only books for teaching the children – mainly from India and Pakistan, Poland and Cyprus – were intended for teaching English to new Australians! The book had a map of Australia and was full of kangaroos!"

"As I got to know some of the pupils who could already speak English, I would visit their homes, they introduced me to the Sikh temple and they tried to teach me to cook Indian food."

In the summer of 1964, the country was entering a general election; the Conservatives had been in power for thirteen years and Macmillan had famously declared 'most of our people have never had it so good'. But not all. Immigration from the Commonwealth, housing shortages and rising unemployment, combined with cynical political opportunism made Smethwick the epicentre of a debate on race. The 1964 campaign in Smethwick has been called 'the most racist election in British history'."

"Every week there was a scare-story…there was a rent strike in one of the new tower blocks when the first immigrant moved in, similarly a bus drivers' strike when a black conductor was going to be made a driver…it was absolutely visceral."

Enter Atam on a Vespa

Amidst this febrile atmosphere Sylvia met her Indian-born husband. She had been invited to help form a multi-racial youth club and it was there that she met Atam Vetta, who had escaped from India at the time of partition.

"He was a Hindu caught on the wrong side of the border. He escaped to Ethiopia where he taught for a while and later settled in Nuneaton where he worked to save money to pay the fees for his PhD. We'd arranged to meet at the Sikh temple at two o'clock, one Sunday to talk about this youth club, I had never met Atam before, and he came along on a Vespa! In 1963 the coolest thing was to turn up on an Italian motorbike…he hasn't lived up to it since mind you! Our relationship had to become serious very quickly because of the circumstances."

Fighting racial prejudice

In that 1964 general election, the openly racist views of the Tory challenger, Peter Griffiths, were widely condemned but the Labour candidate was ineffective. "Atam and I joined the Labour party and we went out with the Labour candidate Patrick Gordon Walker and tried to help him attract the Asian vote. Atam could speak Hindu, Urdu and Punjabi and so he could translate, but Walker was very weak when challenged about racism in the street". Walker's ability to challenge his opponent's racist views was blunted by his political past. As Secretary for the Commonwealth in 1948 he had been responsible for the tribal leader Seretse Kharma's enforced exile from his homeland of Botswana for marrying a white English woman (dramatised in the movie *A United Kingdom*).

Griffiths won the seat, a result that was unique in a general election where every other seat that changed hands passed from Conservative to Labour. Labour came to power under Harold Wilson with a weak majority. "Eighteen months later the seat was won back for Labour by Andrew Faulds, the former actor, who was completely different. He was huge and wonderful. There had been a colour bar at the Labour club, but he refused to cross the threshold unless it was dropped. He wanted to come to our wedding but we were a bit shy, because it wasn't a posh wedding at all."

"After we got married in 1966 we bought a house in Handsworth...a beautiful area but totally neglected. I taught for a year in a class of forty! About half the kids were black and half were white and they played together, no problems. We were there when Enoch Powell made his infamous 'Rivers of Blood' speech and within a couple of days you had the black kids on one side of the playground and the white kids on the other, it was heartbreaking."

Atam's new job as a lecturer at the new Oxford Polytechnic brought the family to Oxford. But despite his expertise in mathematics, his qualifications and experience Atam found it difficult to progress in his career. As Sylvia put it "While outwardly Oxford can seem a lot more civilized, there is still an underlying prejudice."

Kennington connection

Sylvia had given up work when her first child, Justin was born, and the family settled in Kennington. Two more boys, Adrian and Paul, followed in quick succession and Sylvia concentrated on making their tumbledown house livable. As the children grew up Sylvia became more involved in village life. She co-founded the first Mother and Toddler Group in Oxfordshire, meeting in the old wooden village hall in Kennington; was one of the founding members of the Kennington Amateur Dramatic Society, and as chair of Friend of Kennington Library fought a long and successful campaign to save that vital local resource from closure.

Sylvia has been chair of Kennington Overseas Aid for sixteen of its forty-eight years of activity which every year raises funds for overseas development projects. Marilyn Farr, the co-chair of KOA, describes Sylvia as "a force of nature, full of hugely imaginative ideas and the dynamism with which to carry them through…always on the lookout for people who have something useful to offer her various projects and once you're drawn into her net it's difficult to struggle free again. But it's always in a good cause!"

Tex-Mex Sylvia?

Sylvia returned to teaching but had an urge to be her own boss and start a business. Astonishingly this nearly resulted in Oxford's first Mexican fast food restaurant. "I thought tacos would go down great with the students in Oxford!" she told me. Ultimately though the banks were less impressed with the idea and instead she and her business partner Gill Hedge began to run a regular fleamarket out of the Clarendon Press centre on Walton Street. Gradually the business

expanded to include venues in Witney and Didcot. "I'd always been interested in art and art history and so I decided to try and learn more."

When they lost the Walton Street venue they moved to a basement in George Street where they opened Oxford Antiques Omnibus, followed by the Old Jam Factory where Sylvia managed several dealers and a café. As she became better known in the trade she was elected chair of the Thames Valley Art and Antiques Dealers Association. It was during this period that Tim Metcalfe, then deputy editor of *Oxfordshire Limited Edition*, approached her to write a regular column about antiques.

"I'd always dabbled in writing, but I had never taken it seriously. I understand the hurdles disadvantaged kids have to face. If things are not quite in your experience, you don't think they are for you. So, even though I loved writing I couldn't envisage someone from my background being a professional writer."

The art of the interview

"I've always been a bit subversive, and textiles were always rather like a second-class citizen in the antiques trade, so I made my very first feature on textiles! I think they liked it but I still had a lot to learn and Tim took me under his wing." Other series on the theme of antiques followed before Sylvia came up with the idea for *Oxford Castaways*.

"It really started as a continuation of the antiques page but gradually it became more about the castaways themselves." And it's been a really good experience, they are an amazing group of people and I have become friends with many of them. I believe this is very much due to Sylvia's skill as an interviewer. "Sylvia is an irrepressibly optimistic, generous but determined lady with a great knack for getting interviewees to 'open up' naturally," says James Harrison, publisher of 2 of the Castaways compendiums.

"It must seem strange – pathetic even but I have chosen a pair of damaged vases to take to Oxtopia. However they bring together important elements in my life. I was never that interested in what something was worth, but much more in what it tells you about the time and society it comes from. It helps you understand what life was like. One of my first magazine series was Every Antique Tells a Story and I began with the tale behind my vases. It is a tale of political intrigue, alchemy and kidnapping. Porcelain was the most desirable must-have commodity of the seventeenth century. All over Europe attempts were made to copy the amazing Chinese invention. My vases were a failed attempt by a Dutchman who named himself Petrus Van Marum. But his 'soft paste' version copied a Chinese shape and design." In a way these vases connect the dots in Sylvia's story. "I love art, history and story-telling and for me these vases represent all of them."

Brushstrokes in Time

Sylvia's fascination with China has led to her latest novel *Brushstrokes in Time*. It's a haunting love story breaching a silence between a mother and daughter and told against a background of real events during the Cultural Revolution in the 1970s.

"*Brushstrokes in Time* was inspired by an exhibition by the Chinese artist Qu Leilei. He told me the story of the Stars Arts Movement in China in the 1970s. I'd never heard of it but I found it so inspiring that I wanted to write about it. Originally I was going to write it as non-fiction but it was suggested I do a creative writing course, and that gave me the courage to think I could actually write fiction. So Qu Leilei's story (see 3:19) inspired the background of the novel."

The title of the exhibition that first inspired Sylvia to write *Brushstrokes in Time* was "Everyone's life is an epic", and perhaps this sums up not only Sylvia's own approach to life but why *Oxford Castaways* has proved to be such an enduring and rewarding experience both for her and for her readers.

She has one more item to show me. It is a coloured photograph on her wall of a young boy dressed in Indian clothes. "We don't have a single picture of Atam as a child, the first one is of him teaching as an adult. But it was the fashion in the late 19th century to dress up your child and photograph him as a little rajah. Gill, my friend and business partner at the Jam Factory found it in an auction in Dorset and I must have told her I had never seen a picture of him as a little boy...so now this hangs on the walls and I pretend it's Atam as a kid!"

As Sylvia departs for Oxtopia I leave the last word to Sylvia's fellow Castaway Bill Heine (1:3), who she credits with helping transform the series from one about antiques, to one about people:

"Sylvia is the sort of person that 'gets things done'. She will be the source of energy in Oxtopia, the sun around which it revolves. She'll organise all the other castaways so cleverly they won't even know what hit them.

Sylvia Vetta

Born: 1945

Occupation: Creator of Oxford Castaways and Oxtopia, author and tour de force

Castaway Items: Coloured photograph of a young boy dressed as a rajah; 2 Dutch-imitation Chinese vases (damaged)

Original OLE Interview: November 2016

Brushstrokes In Time is published by Claret Press and is also an Essential Audiobook

Oxford Castaways 1 and 2

In 2008, I embarked on a mission to maroon remarkable people on a desert island for *Oxfordshire Limited Edition*.

I asked them to choose an antique, work of art or book to take with them.

After six months, the antique became an object and the magazine features focused on the lives of the castaways.

The upshot, after I sent my 50th castaway to the island of Oxtopia in 2012, was my illustrated book called *Oxford Castaways* followed in 2014 by *Oxford Castaways 2* with a further 40 profiles.

If you have enjoyed *Oxford Castaways 3* and would like to purchase the previous editions go to www.sylviavetta.co.uk or visit my facebook page.

Sylvia Vetta

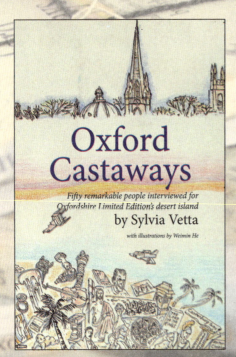

Oxford Castaways
ISBN 978-1-78018-520-0
162pp/£8.99

Oxford Castaways 2
ISBN 978-0-9567-405-6-4
208pp/£9.99

www.oxfordfolio.co.uk